'The theory takes on a new life of its own, more practical, more inspiring.' – *Bill P⸋ Theory, Lafayette, Colorado, USA*

'This short book gives an accessible accoun⸋ of Levels (MOL), a distinctive and pragmat⸋ simple enough to make you wonder why ⸋ profound enough to change what you notice and what you do in therapy.' – *William B. Stiles, Professor Emeritus, Miami University, Oxford, Ohio, USA; President-elect (2012), President (2013) American Psychological Association, Division 29 (Psychotherapy)*

'The hallmark of all living things is that they are self-organising to achieve goals – survival and reproduction in the first instance. Goals of course can also be in conflict, creating disorganisation. In this landmark book, Mansell, Carey and Tai describe Perceptual Control Theory to explore these issues and as a way of taking a transdiagnostic and goal-oriented approach to mental health problems and therapy. Highly accessible and innovative, the book brings many fresh insights to old problems. A book of high quality, scholarship and usefulness, this volume is a delight to read and learn from.' – *Paul Gilbert, OBE, Professor of Clinical Psychology, University of Derby; Past President of the British Association of Behavioural and Cognitive Psychotherapies; Fellow of the British Psychological Society*

'This book provides an innovative and effective new approach to understanding psychopathology and treatment. Based on Perceptual and Control Theory, Method of Levels helps the clinician implement questions and interventions that allow more flexible and effective control for clients, tune in to what is going on in the present moment, relate one level of behavior to higher levels of goals, while helping clients pursue purpose beyond the current "symptom". The verbatim dialogues give the reader wonderful examples of precisely what can be done and how clients respond. Written in a clear and practical style, this book will help clinicians from all CBT models. I highly recommend this valuable book.' – *Robert L. Leahy, Clinical Professor of Psychology, Department of Psychiatry, Weill-Cornell University Medical College, New York; Director, American Institute for Cognitive Therapy; Past-President, Association for Behavioral and Cognitive Therapies*

'This is a wonderful book; intelligent, accessible, innovative and useful. It should be invaluable reading for anyone who wishes to improve their understanding of the human mind or to improve their effectiveness as a therapist.' – *Peter Kinderman, Professor of Clinical Psychology, University of Liverpool*

'This book describes a revolution in psychotherapy. It describes how Powers' rigorous model of mental life is applied to psychopathology through the visionary casework of Tim Carey. The Method of Levels can be used in a pure form or as a technique within CBT and other therapies when there seems little prospect of further progress. The contents are challenging and will require further empirical support but the clinical applications are compelling. My personal experience is that there is something here of great value and that this volume should be widely read and debated. Researchers and clinicians alike should buy this book.' – *Doug Turkington, Honorary Professor of Psychosocial Psychiatry, Institute of Neuroscience, Newcastle University*

'This book is a refreshing addition to the literature on psychological treatments for mental disorders, in that it goes beyond disease entities, adopting rather what is termed a "transdiagnostic" approach to human maladies; and that it goes beyond the ubiquitous cognitive behaviour therapy, building on the core thereof but offering new flexibility and understandings within the Method of Levels paradigm. It covers theoretical and practical aspects of the model, making it an ideal reference source as well as a clinical guide.' – *David Castle, Professor and Chair of Psychiatry, St Vincent's Hospital and The University of Melbourne*

'A truly insightful, important book. A "must read" for all who seek to understand themselves and other people better, particularly those whose lives have been touched by depression, anxiety and stress.' – *Allison Harvey, Professor of Clinical Psychology, University of California, Berkeley*

'Perceptual control theory and the associated "Method of Levels" therapy is a new form of cognitive behaviour therapy designed to help "people to reflect on their thinking and behaviour in a way that helps them become more flexible and adept at reducing their own distress." (p.2). New forms of talking therapy are much needed to help those that do not find current treatments acceptable or effective. Method of Levels treatment is designed for all forms of mental health problems, and such a "transdiagnostic" approach will help to ensure that it is implemented in clinical practice. The authors are to be commended on advancing the field with such an authoritative book on both perceptual control theory and its therapeutic implications." – *Roz Shafran, Professor of Evidence-Based Psychological Treatment, University of Reading, UK*

'A refreshing manual that presents a thought-provoking look behind the scenes of therapeutic change. This very readable, informed text is both theoretically coherent and unashamedly practical. It dares to suggest that the truth – about the shared process of psychological change of all psychological therapies – might actually be out there!' – *Terry Hanley, PhD, Editor of* Counselling Psychology Review; *Research Lead for the Division of Counselling Psychology, British Psychological Society*

'A great achievement! Every therapist should read this book. The Method of Levels is a very clever method to alleviate distress and offers a very interesting promise to boost the development of cognitive behavioural therapy, both in practice and in research.' – *Miguel M. Gonçalves, Professor of Psychology, University of Minho, Portugal; Associate Editor of* Psychotherapy Research

'This is a an excellent book that introduces a break-through advancement of Cogntive Behavioral Therapy (CBT), the most effective psychological treatment. Using a control theory approach to CBT, the authors clearly outline a transdiagnostic form of psychotherapy that targets the distress that arises when people cannot reach their goals in life. This is a must-read text for every practicing clinician and an important book for every therapist in training.' – *Stefan G. Hofmann, PhD, Author of* An Introduction to Modern CBT *(Wiley-Blackwell); Professor of Psychology, Department of Psychology, Boston University*

A Transdiagnostic Approach to CBT using Method of Levels Therapy

Cognitive Behavioural Therapy (CBT) is the treatment of choice for most mental health problems. Each different problem is usually treated by a different model of CBT. Yet evidence tells us that the same processes are responsible for long-term distress in us all. This handy manual draws on evidence and theory to provide the key principles to aid change and recovery.

The transdiagnostic approach is supported by a wealth of evidence that processes such as worry, emotion suppression, self-criticism and avoidance maintain distress across psychological disorders. Perceptual Control Theory (PCT) explains all of these processes as forms of 'inflexible control', and Method of Levels Therapy (MOL) helps people to let go of these habits. The principles and techniques of MOL are clearly and practically described for clinicians to offer a transdiagnostic CBT that is tailor-made to the goals of each client.

This novel volume will be essential reading for novice and experienced CBT therapists, as well as counsellors and psychotherapists. Its accessible explanation of Perceptual Control Theory and its application to real world problems also makes it a useful resource for undergraduates, graduates, and researchers in psychology.

Warren Mansell is a Reader in Psychology, Accredited Cognitive Behavioural Therapist, and Chartered Clinical Psychologist. He has authored over 100 publications on CBT and in 2011 received the May Davidson Award from the British Psychological Society for an outstanding contribution to the field of clinical psychology in the first ten years since qualifying.

Timothy A. Carey is the Associate Professor in Mental Health at the Centre for Remote Health in Alice Springs, Australia. He has been using the Method of Levels in a variety of settings for over ten years and has researched and published extensively on its use.

Sara J. Tai is a Senior Lecturer in Clinical Psychology at the University of Manchester, Chartered Clinical Psychologist and Accredited Cognitive Behavioural Therapist. She is an experienced researcher, practitioner, trainer and supervisor of Cognitive Behaviour Therapies, including the Method of Levels.

Cognitive behaviour therapy (CBT) occupies a central position in the move towards evidence-based practice and is frequently used in the clinical environment. Yet there is no one universal approach to CBT and clinicians speak of first-, second- and even third-wave approaches.

This series provides straightforward, accessible guides to a number of CBT methods, clarifying the distinctive features of each approach. The series editor, Windy Dryden, successfully brings together experts from each discipline to summarise the 30 main aspects of their approach divided into theoretical and practical features.

The CBT Distinctive Features Series will be essential reading for psychotherapists, counsellors, and psychologists of all orientations who want to learn more about the range of new and developing cognitive behaviour approaches.

Titles in the series:
Acceptance and Commitment Therapy by Paul E. Flaxman, J.T. Blackledge and Frank W. Bond
Beck's Cognitive Therapy by Frank Wills
Behavioural Activation by Jonathan W. Kanter, Andrew M. Busch and Laura C. Rusch
Constructivist Psychotherapy by Robert A. Neimeyer
Dialectical Behaviour Therapy by Michaela A. Swales and Heidi L. Heard
Functional Analytic Psychotherapy by Mavis Tsai, Robert J. Kohlenberg, Jonathan W. Kanter, Gareth I. Holman and Mary Plummer Loudon
Metacognitive Therapy by Peter Fisher and Adrian Wells
Mindfulness-Based Cognitive Therapy by Rebecca Crane
Rational Emotive Behaviour Therapy by Windy Dryden
Schema Therapy by Eshkol Rafaeli, David P. Bernstein and Jeffrey Young

For further information about this series please visit
www.routledgementalhealth.com/cbt-distinctive-features

A Transdiagnostic Approach to CBT using Method of Levels Therapy

Distinctive Features

Warren Mansell,
Timothy A. Carey,
and Sara J. Tai

Routledge
Taylor & Francis Group
LONDON AND NEW YORK

First published 2013
by Routledge
27 Church Road, Hove, East Sussex BN3 2FA

Simultaneously published in the USA and Canada
by Routledge
711 Third Avenue, New York, NY 10017

Routledge is an imprint of the Taylor & Francis Group, an informa business

© 2013 Warren Mansell, Timothy A. Carey and Sara J. Tai

The right of Warren Mansell, Timothy A. Carey and Sara J. Tai to be identified as authors of this work has been asserted by them in accordance with sections 77 and 78 of the Copyright, Designs and Patents Act 1988.

All rights reserved. No part of this book may be reprinted or reproduced or utilised in any form or by any electronic, mechanical, or other means, now known or hereafter invented, including photocopying and recording, or in any information storage or retrieval system, without permission in writing from the publishers.

Trademark notice: Product or corporate names may be trademarks or registered trademarks, and are used only for identification and explanation without intent to infringe.

British Library Cataloguing in Publication Data
A catalogue record for this book is available from the British Library

Library of Congress Cataloging in Publication Data
Mansell, Warren.
A transdiagnostic approach to CBT using method of levels therapy : distinctive features / Warren Mansell, Timothy A. Carey, and Sara Tai.
  p. cm. — (Cognitive behaviour therapy distinctive features)
Includes bibliographical references and index.
1. Cognitive therapy. 2. Psychotherapy. I. Carey, Timothy A. II. Tai, Sara.
III. Title.
RC489.C63M32 2012
616.89'1425—dc23

2012019165

ISBN: 978–0–415–50763–9 (hbk)
ISBN: 978–0–415–50764–6 (pbk)
ISBN: 978–0–203–08133–4 (ebk)

Typeset in Times
by RefineCatch Ltd, Bungay, Suffolk

Contents

Acknowledgements   xiii

Introduction   1

Part 1 THEORY   5
1. Thinking styles and behaviours that maintain psychological distress are transdiagnostic   7
2. Transdiagnostic processes overlap to form a core process that maintains distress   11
3. The phenomenon of control: perception, comparison and action   15
4. The control of perception: not the control of behaviour   21
5. The negative feedback loop   25
6. Basic causes of the loss of control   29
7. Hierarchies of control: going up and down levels   31
8. Conflict   35
9. Reorganisation: a non-linear process of change   41
10. Awareness and imagination   45

11 Arbitrary (or inflexible) control maintains distress via conflict	49
12 Directing awareness to regain flexible control: a common factor of CBT, effective therapy and natural recovery	53
13 Interpersonal control	55
14 Circular causality and model building	57
15 It's all perception	61

Part 2 PRACTICE 63

16 The setting conditions: a problem that the client is willing to talk about	65
17 The stance: to enable the client's flexible control as efficiently as possible	69
18 Method of Levels goal one: asking about the current problem	73
19 Method of Levels goal two: asking about disruptions	79
20 Using the past, controlling the present, and living for the future	83
21 'Green Apples': working through problems without disclosure	89
22 What to say at the first session	93
23 How much treatment and how often to provide it	97
24 A focus on distress rather than symptoms	101
25 Outcome monitoring	107
26 Evaluating your own practice	111
27 The therapeutic relationship: liberated exploration	115
28 Building MOL into other therapies and therapeutic practices	121
29 Utilising control theory in existing CBT	127
30 Interventions without talking: testing the controlled variable	133

Appendix 1: MOL evaluation forms	137
Appendix 2: Method of Levels Adherence Scale (MOLAS: Version 3)	143
Appendix 3: Method of Levels: common questions about the therapy	153
Further resources	159
Bibliography	161
Index	167

Acknowledgements

We would like to thank Windy Dryden for commissioning this manual, taking his lead from the clinical researchers who have opened the door for transdiagnostic approaches to CBT – Allison Harvey, Ed Watkins, Roz Shafran, David Barlow, Bob Leahy, and David A. Clark. We have a deep gratitude and respect for the innovator of PCT and the initial developer of MOL – William T. Powers – for his tireless work spanning seven decades, his support with the work leading up to this book, and his pithy emails of insight and encouragement. We also thank the practitioners of MOL in the early days – Margaret Carey, Richard and Gillian Mullan, Chris and Margaret Spratt – for testing the fruits of this approach many years ago, and we thank the increasing numbers of clinicians who are taking up MOL in their practices. In particular, we thank Phil McEvoy and the team at Six Degrees Social Enterprise for embracing our ideas for theory and practice, adapting them in their service, supporting our research, and broadening the application of this approach within primary care. Thank you to the young researchers and clinicians who have contributed to the evaluation of MOL at the University of Manchester, piloted our training and supervision, and contributed research findings, materials, and ideas to this book – Rebecca Kelly (therapeutic relationship), Miriam Samad (questions about MOL), Lydia Morris (group therapy), Timothy Bird (coding of MOL sessions), Marijke Lansbergen, Amy Hamilton, Savas Akgonul, Carolyn Waterhouse, Vaneeta Sadhnani, and Sally Higginson.

Introduction

This book is about understanding people. Whether or not you have experienced mental health problems, or whether or not you work within mental health services, the principles we outline here can be applied to understanding the ways in which all people think, feel, and behave in a whole range of situations and contexts. These principles apply to all living beings. But equally, the very same principles can help to clarify what can happen when people do develop problems with their mental well-being. We outline the processes that can determine whether these are transient difficulties that resolve in the short term, or the kind of experiences that can evolve into long lasting residual problems. We also describe a way of helping people move forward and achieve a greater sense of purpose and well-being in their lives. Again, these methods can work for anyone who wants to increase their self-awareness and control over their lives.

The ideas put forward in this book are based on a theory known as Perceptual Control Theory (PCT), which was developed by William T. Powers throughout the 1950s up to the present day (1973; 2005). Put simply, PCT is an explanation of behaviour, and the goals which are important to us, associated with all our different levels of behaviour. In other words, PCT says that our actions in life can be understood as part of an ongoing process of creating, achieving, and maintaining our goals. Distress is what happens when we cannot reach those goals.

The Method of Levels (MOL) is a transdiagnostic form of Cognitive Behaviour Therapy (CBT): a direct application of PCT. MOL encourages people to reflect on their thinking and behaviour in a way that helps them to become more flexible and adept at reducing their own distress. Manoeuvring attention to develop awareness of important personal goals and increasing capacity for mental flexibility are key processes we will be explaining as part of this therapy. MOL is a type of talking therapy, which can be used to treat a wide range of difficulties, especially for people who might present to mental health services. It might also be applied usefully within other contexts; for example, schools, and workplaces, and within all sorts of interpersonal situations where people need to be understood.

People often know what it is they want to be doing or where they want to be going, but for some reason they cannot get there. MOL is a way of helping people to consider what the goals behind their actions are and explore the reasons preventing them from living the life they want. Often people are not fully aware of the other goals they have in the background, even though these can interfere with the goal they are currently pursuing. MOL is a way of helping people to focus on what is going on right now and talk about problems as they experience them in the present. By doing so, it is possible to direct their awareness to other things that are going on in the background competing for their attention.

This book is presented in two parts – first, an overview of the main principles of PCT and how these can provide a general framework for understanding people. In the second half we focus more on the application of these principles to practice and, more specifically, how to use MOL as a psychological intervention for distress that can also lead to a wide range of mental health problems. We have provided a variety of practical examples and vignettes, based upon the experiences we have had through both our clinical practice and the research we have conducted. By using PCT as a framework, we describe MOL as a psychological process, which emphasises placing the client at the heart of the therapy and the change process, within their own time frame. Our aim is to detail the fundamental principles involved in any successful therapy or change process.

With the broadening array of psychological approaches that exists nowadays, we are aware that terminology has evolved to mean many different things within different contexts. Within this book, we undoubtedly will require the use of language, such as the words 'goals' and 'control'; which may have alternative meanings and connotations, depending on your theoretical background and orientation. We have tried to define the principles behind the terms we use, and request that you overlook the limitations of the language we employ in favour of focusing on the important principles we aim to convey.

We have come to PCT and MOL from a background in cognitive and behavioural therapies, as well as a depth of experience in other frameworks and contexts, such as psychodynamic therapy, behavioural analysis, metacognitive therapy, compassionate mind approaches and working within schools and higher education systems. We have found in PCT and MOL a way of crystallising our knowledge of psychological interventions, developing new insights and refining our techniques. When our previous training has proved hard to implement, we have seen the benefits in understanding 'control' in our clients, ourselves and the therapeutic relationship. The aim of this book is to provide you with some of these opportunities. We hope that the manual is up to the task and look forward to hearing from you if you plan to take this approach forward in your own work, or have constructive criticism of the therapy and how to implement it.

Part 1

THEORY

PART 1: THEORY

Thinking styles and behaviours that maintain psychological distress are transdiagnostic

The transdiagnostic approach is an empirical exercise to demonstrate that there are thinking styles and behaviours responsible for maintaining psychological disorders, and that these factors are shared across all disorders. It proposes that CBT, and other interventions, can be effective by targeting these factors directly, without necessarily using information about a person's diagnosis – their 'disorder(s)'.

The transdiagnostic approach does not claim that therapy will necessarily be more efficacious if applied across disorders – it may simply be more efficient and easier to train and disseminate.

To be viable, the transdiagnostic approach does not necessarily need to challenge the reliability and validity of the established classification systems for categorising psychiatric disorders. However, it does pose questions about the usefulness of the established classification systems that we have inherited. In many other areas of science – such as biology, chemistry, and physics – categorisation is based upon classification schemes that are underpinned by recognised causal mechanisms. The primary purpose of scientific inquiry is to obtain knowledge about underlying causal mechanisms. The most critical advances in science typically come from identifying causal mechanisms and gaining an understanding of how they work – for example, the molecular bonds between the atoms that hold chemical compounds together and the natural selection that underlies the evolution of living organisms. How far would Galileo have got if he had been focused upon the differences between the objects he dropped from the Leaning Tower of Pisa rather than looking for the causal mechanism which explained why the objects fell like they did? Most likely he would have developed a different set of principles for each object, and been none the wiser as to how gravity operates. We propose that the historical development of arbitrary classification schemes has hindered the development of the social sciences, and the understanding of the psychological factors that affect mental health in particular.

Since the early disciplines of psychotherapy emerged, many of the key processes and mechanisms identified by psychiatrists, psychologists, and counsellors have had a 'transdiagnostic' character. In fact, we could call these 'pre-diagnostic' or 'universal' when describing approaches that preceded the modern diagnostic system. However, these early disciplines lost credibility as they failed to establish the relationship between the causal mechanisms and the empirical evidence that was available. The transdiagnostic application of CBT, on the other hand, has validated a universal approach to understanding psychological distress by closely examining the vast amount of research conducted on different diagnostic groups. It has identified the mechanisms that explain why psychological distress persists in these different 'disorders'. In the pivotal book that launched this approach (Harvey *et al.* 2004), Allison Harvey led the conscious decision to articulate these mechanisms, and the systematic review that followed highlighted some important ideas about how CBT could be practised. We are now developing these ideas.

In sum, Harvey *et al.* found that a total of 12 thinking styles and behaviours were shared across all of the adult psychological disorders studied, and a further nine were possible candidates awaiting additional evidence. Only two of all the processes studied (jumping to conclusions and external attribution of blame) could have been specific to 'psychotic disorders', but even these spanned a range of psychotic disorders and did not appear to be unique to any one of them (Corcoran *et al.* 2008). Since 2004, the research literature has provided yet further support for the approach (e.g. Ehring and Watkins 2008; McManus *et al.* 2010). Indeed, one might suggest that the onus is on researchers of disorder-specific approaches to demonstrate that the processes implicated in their models are unique to particular disorders. One likely compromise is that some transdiagnostic processes, like worry for example, are elevated in their frequency, impact, and distress in some disorder categories, such as generalised anxiety disorder (Brown *et al.* 1992).

While the results of the Harvey *et al.* review set the stage for a transdiagnostic CBT, the exercise was deliberately empirical in its emphasis. The many thinking styles and behaviours were taken largely at face value and no serious attempt was made to identify how the causal mechanisms 'thought suppression', 'experiential avoidance', and 'safety-seeking behaviours' might operate. An initial attempt was made by Harvey *et al.* to demonstrate how formulation and treatment could proceed using a transdiagnostic approach. Yet, the authors acknowledged that a more parsimonious account would be necessary to drive research and treatment for the future.

PART 1: THEORY

2

Transdiagnostic processes overlap to form a core process that maintains distress

The field of CBT and, in turn, psychotherapy as a whole, utilises diverse terminology. The desire for leaders in the field to develop their own niche therapy with its own jargon is palpable. Walter Mischel, former president of the Association of Psychological Science, calls it the 'toothbrush problem' – like toothbrushes, everyone wants their own and no one wants to share! Indeed, a task force, sponsored by 12 international organisations, is developing a lexicon for a shared language for different approaches in an attempt to try to describe and simplify the wide range of therapies – www.commonlanguagepsychotherapy.org. At the last count, over 90 therapies were registered.

In a similar vein, in the last chapter we pointed out that over 20 cognitive and behavioural processes are potentially transdiagnostic. Are these different from one another in any significant ways? Later, we shall see that the answer is maybe 'no' when it comes to explaining why problems exist.

A linchpin of the control theory approach to transdiagnostic CBT is that it is highly likely that the transdiagnostic processes that have been identified overlap to form a core process that maintains distress. This would give us a much more parsimonious account of the basic principles of how the mind works, and how it gets into distress, than the myriad of different models, explanations, and increasingly complex descriptions that we currently have. We wonder whether the complexity in many of our current models has more to do with the way we are approaching the problem than anything inherent in the problem itself. Taking the field of astronomy as an example, there was a time when the orbits of celestial bodies seemed strange and mysterious and ever increasingly complex models were developed to account for the paths they seemed to travel. The difficulty, however, was that astronomers were observing the planets from the perspective that the earth was at the centre of the solar system. When our understanding changed from a geocentric to a heliocentric solar system, the orbits of the planets were much easier to understand. This illustrates how any phenomenon can seem complex before it is accurately understood. Returning to the field of mental health, what evidence is there that the thinking styles and behaviours that enforce people's problems are related in a simple way?

Typically, clinical researchers try to point out the differences between the process they are proposing and those identified by other researchers (Mansell 2008). Yet, when they do the opposite, and look for overlaps between them, the similarities seem increasingly evident.

Studies of this kind have been conducted on students (Aldao and Nolen-Hoeksema 2010; Bird *et al.* 2012; Field and Cartwright-Hatton 2008), bipolar clients (Schwannauer 2007), clients with physical illnesses (Bird *et al.* 2012), and mixed primary and secondary care clients (Patel 2010). In every study, the shared component, of between two and eighteen different cognitive and behavioural processes, has correlated with psychological distress. Typically, processes that are shared across problems are more predictive of distress than any of the individual processes specific to one problem. This occurs even though the processes are hugely diverse and may even seem to be opposite from one another. For example, they include suppressing thoughts and dwelling on negative thoughts excessively; focusing on threats in the environment and focusing excessively on oneself; behaviours directed outwards like using alcohol to suppress feelings, and behaviours directed inwards like self-critical thinking. A core process may unite all of these transdiagnostic processes that account for these diverse manifestations of distress and the apparent contradictions that they present.

A control theory approach to CBT is distinctive in that no single behaviour or thinking style is emphasised as maintaining psychological distress. Instead, control theory proposes that it is how any process relates to a person's own unique, personal goals – essentially how much it conflicts with them and a limited awareness of this conflict on the part of the client – that is the problem. Effective therapy expands this awareness.

In the following chapters, we will set the foundations to explain this core mechanism within mental health problems in much more detail for you to see the direct and transparent link to clinical practice. The first step we need to take is to provide an account of what we mean by 'control'.

PART 1: THEORY

3

The phenomenon of control: perception, comparison and action

Even though psychology is commonly described as the science of behaviour, specifying just what exactly 'behaviour' is has been troublesome. There have been attempts to define behaviour in terms of observable and measurable actions or deeds, however, this seems to exclude a large proportion of otherwise important human activity, such as reflecting, thinking, daydreaming, planning, and so on. Attempts to correct this by creating more expansive definitions have not really removed the conundrum. It makes it difficult to conduct scientific activity when the core phenomenon is not easily defined or identified.

Around the middle of the last century, a physicist and control systems engineer by the name of William T. Powers noticed that the servomechanisms he was working on seemed, at times, almost as though they were alive. In particular, the way they could vary their output to counteract the effects of unpredictable environmental disturbances in order to keep the input detected by the sensors matching a pre-specified standard was uncannily like human behaviour. A household-heating thermostat will produce more or less heat, depending on the fluctuating temperature of the room or house in order to keep the temperature it detects matching the temperature that has been set. A person will sit closer to the fire, put on another sweater, or perhaps open a window in order to keep their body temperature feeling the way they like. Similarly, a cruise control system on a car will accelerate and decelerate according to the changing gradient of the road in order to keep the car travelling at the speed the driver has set. It is almost as though the driver's foot is still on the accelerator pedal; such is the accurate mimicking that the cruise control system can do.

Powers noticed that the similarities between the behaviour of these machines and human behaviour reflected a common underlying property. That property was the phenomenon of control. Control can be considered to be a phenomenon of nature in the same way that lightning, magnetism or gravity is. Control, however, is a phenomenon that is peculiar to living things. In fact, the 'living' that a living thing does is a process of control. One of the most fundamental differences between living things and non-living things is that living things control and non-living things do not (except for the non-living things that have been designed to control but even then, they do not control autonomously).

If you push on a rock, its movement is determined entirely by its mass and the force applied to it (as well as the surface it is resting on when it is pushed). If you push on a living thing, however, its movement is much less predictable. How it moves, and the way it moves, will be determined by both the force of the push as well as internal states that are affected by the push.

Living things control and non-living things do not. That is a key insight to remember and one that is fundamental to this book. So what is control? Well, although there are formal definitions of control, there are also common understandings. Most people we have asked can offer a definition of control that has something to do with 'making things happen the way you want'.

In some situations 'control' is almost considered to be a 'dirty word' and often people do not like to use the term. 'Control' seems to be associated with being very constrained and deliberate as well as trying to 'boss other people around'. It seems much more fashionable at the moment to talk, instead, about things like 'acceptance'. We think that is unfortunate and stems from a lack of understanding about what control is and how it works. In scientific terms, people who are relaxed and 'go with the flow' control just as much as authoritarian dictators. Their control is simply more flexible and adaptive than the control of rigid 'control freaks'. The only people who do not control are the ones who fill our cemeteries. In fact, anything that is alive, from a single cell to a human being, controls. To put it in biological terms, for an organised constellation of organic matter to be alive and stay alive, it must act on its external environment in order to maintain the integrity of its internal environment. Control really is about life and death. It is that important.

Powers did not simply identify control as a fundamental property of our nature as living beings; he also described how it might work in specific, quantifiable terms. He used the concepts he had taken from control engineering to develop a theoretical explanation of how perceptual experience is organised so that we are to be able to exercise control in our lives. This makes it relatively unique among theories of behaviour. We wonder, in fact, how many theories there would still be if the principles of all theories had to be specified in precise, quantifiable ways so that functional models could be built to simulate the aspect of behaviour being explained by the theory. The first publication of Powers' work dates back to an abstract for The American Psychologist in 1957, with the first full publications three years later (Powers *et al.* 1960a, b). The recognised source of the elaboration of the theory is *Behaviour: The Control of Perception* (Powers 1973; 2005). While Powers was not the first to use control engineering or 'living systems' ideas in the social sciences (e.g. Wiener 1948), his approach is unique in many ways that make it the theory of choice for most social scientists (Powers 1998). Powers' approach became known as Perceptual Control Theory (PCT) in the 1980s. There are actually many different kinds of 'control theory' besides PCT. However, for the sake of simplicity, we will be using the terms PCT and control theory interchangeably. A range of further details about PCT and the evidence base that has been developed since the 1970s are available at www.pctweb.org.

Powers was able to identify three essential components to control: perception, comparison, and action. He suggested that in order for living things to make events happen the way they want, they have to be able to perceive the current situation (experience), they have to be able to compare what is currently being perceived with an internal standard (the way they want it to be), and they have to be able to act (behaviour) on their environment to make what is being perceived match the internal standard. Control theorists call this process negative feedback, which will be described in further detail later on.

The ubiquity of negative feedback that underpins control is such that we can use some very familiar examples to explain PCT. Even nursery rhymes and fairy tales can help! The story of Goldilocks provides a good example of control in action. Goldilocks did not eat the porridge that was too hot or too cold. She ate the porridge that was 'just right'. Similarly she did not sleep in the beds that were too hard or too soft. She slept in the bed that was 'just right'. For Goldilocks to be able to dine on porridge that was 'just right' she had to be able to taste (perceive) the porridge she found, she had to be able to compare it with her idea of the porridge she liked best, and she had to be able to act to make the porridge she was tasting match her ideal porridge. Basically, the idea of control theory is that we all have 'just rights' in our heads for the whole kaleidoscope of experiences that are our lives. When the world we are experiencing matches our 'just rights', then life is good and we act to keep things happening this way. When conditions and circumstances change and our experiences are not 'just right' anymore, we act to bring them back to the way we want them to be.

All significant human behaviour (and that of other living things) can be considered from this perspective. When someone makes a cup of coffee they have to be able to perceive the state of the coffee, compare it to the state they would like (latte, espresso, cappuccino, etc.) and be able to act in order to make what they are currently perceiving (no coffee) be the way they want it to be (double-shot latte). Notice that there are lots of different ways that a person can act in order to make 'no coffee' match 'double-shot latte'. They might make it themselves, or they might ask a friend to make it, or they might go to their favourite cafe. There is more than one way to skin a cat (so the saying goes) and this turns out to be a hallmark of control. Actions vary in order to make what is being experienced (perceived) be the way it is intended. This insight actually emerged at the dawn of empirical psychology (James 1890) but was not formalised in research until the last century (Mansell and Carey 2009). From an insider's perspective, it is the consequences of behaviour that are important, not the behaviour itself.

It is as though, from the time we start living to the time we stop, we have a variety of 'states' in our minds that we seek to create and maintain. These states describe or provide the 'good' life as we experience it. As babies we have only a few states – such as the states of dryness, warmth, closeness, and being full. Even as babies though, there will be variation in these states, for example how full each baby likes to be and how energetically they will work to maintain that level. Growing and maturing involves populating our minds with an increasing number of states. Perhaps that is why stimulation is so important to a growing child. Even here, though, individuals will have preferred states for the amount of stimulation they receive. As adults these states are reflected in the lives we live. We have states about our relationships, our level of activity, how much we achieve, our propensity to collect gadgets, and so on. Differences in human functioning, therefore, can be understood with respect to variation in desired states. A necessary first step, then, in providing assistance to people to live the lives they intend, is to spend time trying to understand some of the important states they are seeking to maintain through utilising their behaviour.

Perhaps this explains why there is so much ambiguity, tentativeness, and uncertainty in psychology specifically and the life sciences more generally. Much of the research conducted to help us understand behaviour has been conducted from the perspective of an external observer. It is very hard to make sense of behaviour from an outsider's vantage point.

While patterns and regularities in behaviour are often only discernible in a probabilistic and statistical sense, the regularities in the consequences of behaviour are much more robust. For example, people get themselves from home to work every day even though the specific actions they use are never exactly the same. If they used the same actions to drive to work on Tuesday that they had used to drive to work on Monday they probably wouldn't get beyond the end of their street. Every day is different in terms of the environmental conditions. There are different cars on the road, you get to the train station at a slightly different time, the bus is running late because of an accident, it's raining and windy, your friend just rang and said that they won't be able to pick you up today, and so on. Yet, despite these differences, people produce the same outcome (arriving at work) over and over again.

Our day-to-day life, therefore, is characterised by making things happen in a consistent and regular way by using actions that are inconsistent and irregular (control). We keep our appearance the way we like it to be, we maintain the friendships that are important to us, and we pursue the career we have mapped out. All of these things require us to be able to constantly vary our behaviour the way we need to so that we continue to perceive things the way we want them to be. You might ask whether perceptions and experiences are really the same thing; we are proposing that any experience can only be based on information, as it is perceived through an individual's senses at any given time. Their perception is therefore their current reality.

Perception, comparison, and action are the three processes that produce control. Control could well be a unifying phenomenon for the life sciences. It is certainly crucial when it comes to understanding and treating psychological problems. As we will explain throughout this book, problems of living are, fundamentally, problems of control. When someone becomes chronically psychologically distressed, control in some way has been disrupted. By approaching the conceptualisation and treatment of psychological problems from the perspective of control, we might achieve greater clarity and resolution for some of the most contentious theoretical issues in psychology. Many of these are covered later and include the debate about common versus specific factors, the 'dodo bird hypothesis' (the idea that all psychotherapy is equally effective), the categorisation of problems into apparently discrete disorders, the mind/body split, the interaction between the environment and the individual's goals, and the divide between psychological and physical problems. Ultimately we might provide treatments that are more effective and more efficient because they will be based on a more accurate depiction of why we act in the ways we do.

PART 1: THEORY

The control of perception: not the control of behaviour

If it seems plausible that control might be important in understanding 'normal' human behaviour as well as the times when behaviour is disrupted, then it is important to spend a little more time clarifying the nature of control. Control is widely discussed in psychology. Ideas about controlling or regulating what we do are common. By and large, however, when control is discussed, it is most often described in the context of producing the right 'output'. You might read, for example, about strategies to produce behavioural, or thought, control, or emotional regulation.

This focus on control of output highlights the important part that functional models can play in scientific progress. Many models exist in psychology at the moment, but they are conceptual models, or perhaps statistical models. Conceptual models are essentially someone's ideas about something that are expressed diagrammatically. Statistical models are usually expressed diagrammatically as well. However, they also usually have numbers that quantify the associations between different variables in the diagram.

A functional model, however, is a much more exacting test of one's ideas about how something works. When a functional model is put together according to a researcher's ideas, the model either works or it doesn't. If it does not work the way the researcher thinks it should, then clearly, the researcher's ideas about the phenomenon under scrutiny need to be revised. We will have some more to say about models later in the book.

This preamble about models is important when discussing the theory of control that Powers developed – PCT. Powers expressed his ideas in such a way that functional models could be built and thus tested. The results were surprising. First, the models produced behaviour that mapped very closely the behaviour that was being explained. Second, the models indicated that when living things control, they do not actually control their output (behaviour); they control their input (perception).

This simple statement has huge implications for psychology. The notion of the control of behaviour is a mainstay of psychological thought. Generally, it is considered that either *external* events and conditions impact on the individual to produce certain behaviours, or *internal* states, such as goals and plans, generate particular behaviours. Powers, however, discovered that behaviour is not what is controlled at all. Rather, the perceptual consequences of behaviour are controlled. We use our behaviour to produce, create, or control what we are sensing, experiencing, and perceiving. Behaviour *is* the control of perception (Powers 1973; 2005).

Some areas of psychology have been very close to this idea for a long time. Concepts such as cognitive dissonance, selective attention, resilience, and internal motivation are all nibbling at the edges of the paradigm of controlled perceptual input. Unfortunately, they have all been conceptualised and researched from a stance of controlled behavioural output so they have not progressed as far as they might have otherwise. The very basis of psychological research in terms of Independent and Dependent Variables (IVs and DVs) is a direct reflection of our allegiance to the model of behavioural control that is based upon linear, as opposed to 'closed loop', thinking (Marken 2009).

The IV–DV relationship is based upon linear thinking and generates law-like regularities (e.g. stimuli are associated with a response) that seem to be based on intuitive common sense. However, it does not stand up to rigorous scrutiny when we closely observe the behaviour of living beings in practice (Pellis and Bell 2011). When computer models of everyday tasks based on PCT are compared to linear models, the PCT models have been found to show a higher level of accuracy in simulating the real behaviour (e.g. Bourbon and Powers 1999). The comparison we are providing here can be illustrated by a simple thought experiment. Consider driving a car. We could think about behaviour in terms of the angle of your foot on the accelerator pedal and the way you position your hands on the steering wheel and move it around. We could think of perception as all the visual information you are receiving as you drive – the position between you and the car in front, where your car is in the lane, where the other cars beside and behind you are, the number that the speedometer needle is pointing to, and so on. When considered in this way, it is easy to appreciate that perception takes precedence over behaviour. You would not arbitrarily decide what position the steering wheel should be in, or you wouldn't arbitrarily choose a particular angle for your foot to depress the accelerator pedal! You move the steering wheel any way you need to in order to keep seeing the car where you want to see it on the road. Similarly you increase and decrease the amount you depress the accelerator pedal to keep your car moving at the speed you want it to move at. Therefore, you use your behaviours (depressing accelerator pedal, moving steering wheel) to make your perceptions (where the car is and how fast it's moving) be right. That is, your behaviours control your perceptions – not the other way around. For those who are interested, this example of driving has been modelled in practice using PCT (Nilsson 2001).

We think that current diagnostic categories are akin to grouping together all the people who drive with two hands at the top of the steering wheel in one category, all the people who drive with only one hand on the steering wheel in another category, all the people who drive with both hands on the sides of the steering wheel in another category, and so on. We might even discover difficulties of 'comorbidity' when some people at some times drive with both their hands on the top of the steering wheel and, at other times, drive with only one hand on the steering wheel. We do not think that grouping people's behaviour in this way is useful, but we do believe that there would be some underlying consistencies that would be instructive. Concerns about safety might be common; having a destination in mind might also be shared. This example might help to illustrate the focus of this book, which is less about specific behaviours and more about the important, common, transdiagnostic underlying processes.

When people access psychological treatment, therefore, it is not help with producing the 'right behaviour' or thinking the 'right thoughts' that they need. Learning how to produce the right output will not be effective for very long or in many situations. People who are psychologically distressed have experiences that are not the way they want them to be and, for some reason, they cannot make them be just right. We propose that effective treatments help people get 'unstuck' and develop new insights, new perspectives, new approaches, and new ways of operating. Sometimes this undoubtedly involves new behaviours, new thoughts, and new feelings. These behaviours, thoughts, and feelings arise, however, as the person regains control over important aspects of their life.

The negative feedback loop

The principles that we have covered already – control; perception, comparison, and action; behaviour as the control of perception – are substantiated within a working unit called the negative feedback loop. We will provide some detail of the theory in this section to illustrate the technical nature of PCT and show how it describes the actual mechanisms underpinning behaviour rather than describing general principles that we typically find in other psychological theories. This, in turn, should help to illustrate later how a fascination with the 'mechanisms' occurring within the mind of the client is part and parcel of the therapy derived from control theory.

This negative feedback loop is actually the fundamental component of a wide range of engineering applications, from a thermostat, to cruise control systems, to the humble flushing toilet. The concept of negative feedback was first discovered in biology in the late nineteenth century by Claude Bernard and adapted by Walter Cannon as *homeostasis*. It was implemented in engineering in the early twentieth century, and then first brought into psychology with the advent of the cybernetic movement (Wiener 1948). Yet the idea was only refined within working models when PCT was developed during the 1950s and 1960s. According to PCT, these negative feedback loops are the 'building blocks' of any living nervous system. We shall cover later how they are organised to implement complex processes of thinking and action.

In a negative feedback loop, the perceptual signal from the environment is compared to an internal reference signal or 'standard' (so in other words, the perceptual signal is reversed by subtracting it from the internal reference signal). The discrepancy between the environmental signal and the internal standard creates an error signal. The error signal then initiates an action that counteracts the disturbances from the environment. The effect is to bring the perception closer to the internal standard, or in everyday language, to bring one's experiences closer towards one's goals.

There are two other features that are critical. First, the action must be significantly stronger than the error signal in order to counteract the effects in the environment causing it. To do this, the error signal is magnified by a factor called the 'gain'. You may be familiar with the term 'gain' from amplifiers used for music performance. This is because amplifiers are built from electrical versions of negative feedback loops. Second, is the 'loop'. One's own actions are connected to one's perception via the environment. This is the feedback process; the closed loop from one's own actions back to one's perception. This feature implements 'behaviour as the control of perception'.

When conducting therapy based on control theory, we assume that a person's thoughts, feelings, and behaviours are all components of closed loops that integrate with their environment. We interact with one another via these connections with the environment we share. This allows us to help one another (when we are incorporated into the feedback of another person by their actions) to collectively control experiences together (when two people share the same goals) or sometimes, conflict with one another (when one person acts as a disturbance to another person's goals).

The negative feedback loop can be explained and modelled to various levels of precision. Here we have explained just some of the components, which are also illustrated in Figure 5.1. When control theory researchers use these negative feedback loops to model real world systems, a range of other components are needed. Many of these are explained in detail in Powers (2008) and in a range of other publications on the theory available at www.pctweb.org. For the sake of this chapter, it is important to know that a working mechanism, called the negative feedback loop, can be used to implement goal-directed, purposeful behaviour. Control theory is a physical theory. This is yet another feature that makes control theory distinctive. It explains through working mechanisms – not through hypothetical verbal explanations. Words can be used to try to communicate the theory, but ultimately an understanding of the theory comes from seeing exactly how it works in practice.

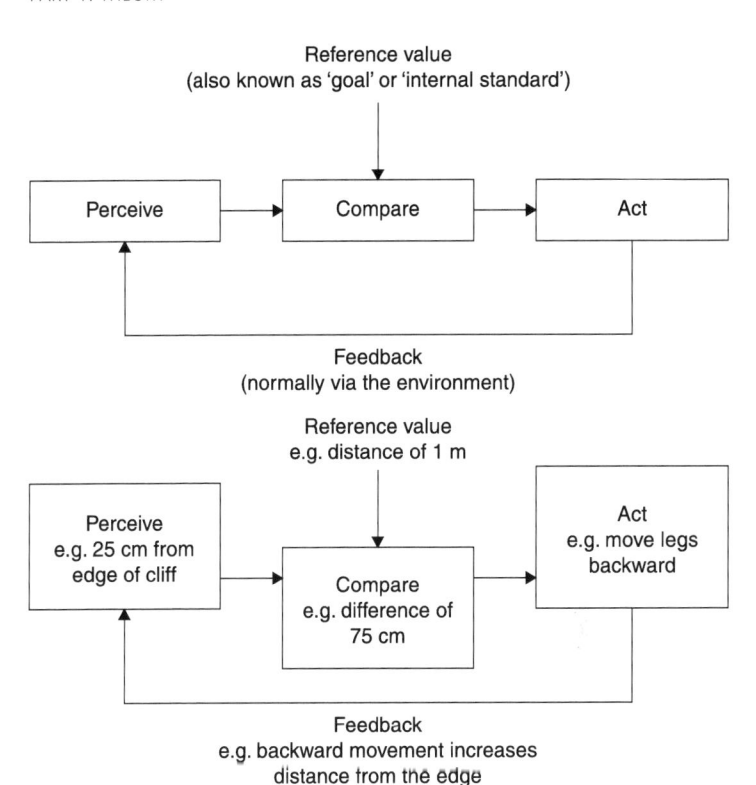

Figure 5.1 Perception, comparison, and action are the three processes that produce control.

Basic causes of the loss of control

The diagram of the closed loop in the last chapter points to how control can be lost, as well as how it can be achieved. If any element of the loop is missing, for a particular experience, then that experience cannot be controlled. Let's take this one point at a time.

First, we need to be able to perceive something to be able to control it. Put simply, to be able to drive along a road, we need to perceive where we are on the road. Distractions can lead to fatal accidents. Within broader areas of our life, in order to be able to feel comfortable or to be liked by another person, we similarly need to pay attention to these perceptions. This means that we are better at controlling when we are attending to our senses and the present moment experience. In this way we can judge whether we are experiencing what we want to experience – being 'just comfortable enough' or 'liked by my friends', for example. So paying attention to current perceptions is important.

Second, we need a reference value for our experience – our internal standard. It is hard to know how to get what we want until we know how much of it we require. To use the driving example, we need a reference value of which side of the road to drive on, how close to be to the curb, and at what speed. In broader examples, we need a sense of how much comfort is OK for us, or how much we want to be liked by our friends. So, being aware of our goals and internal standards is important.

Third, we need some way of acting on our environment to be able to control. Therefore, we need our bodies to be able to act. This is typically through muscular movement – speech, walking, grasping, writing, for example. Each of these actions allows us to control. Without this capacity, we would not be able to control our experiences. However, we might be able to control our reference values for these experiences and imagine them; we return to this capacity later. Essentially, it is important to be able to act in order to control.

Fourth, we need an environment that allows the feedback to occur. When driving a car, if we had a swimming pool underneath the car rather than a road, our actions would be futile. In much broader life goals, we need to have an environment that we can act on and that does not create so much disturbance that our control is completely compromised. For example, children have little control over who their parents are, and many people have little control over where they live and over natural disasters that may affect their lives. So, it is important to identify the aspects of our environment that we can control.

Despite all the above constraints on control, it seems that the human mind is remarkably adept at readjusting and reorganising to find ways of regaining control. For example, people who are partially sighted learn to use touch and hearing to communicate. People with physical disabilities learn to rely on machines, adaptations to buildings, or even help from others to realise their goals. For this reason, it is important to help facilitate people's control using self-generated opportunities and by considering whether they have access to the perceptions, reference values, actions, and environments to do so. Yet, many people still report losing control and purpose in their lives even when these elements seem present, at least from the outsider's perspective. This is most likely due to a different kind of problem – conflict – which we will return to later.

Hierarchies of control: going up and down levels

An elegant feature of PCT is the way in which it can account for differences in behavioural complexity. The closed causal control system operating by negative feedback is considered to be the basic building block from a PCT view of life, while the processes of perception, comparison, and action remain the order of the day throughout the Kingdom of Living Things. Regardless of how simple or complex the behaviour is, a fundamental proposition from PCT is that all behaviour is part of a control process.

The process of control remains constant despite varying behavioural complexities. The reason for differences in behavioural complexity can be accounted for by the types of perceptions that are controlled in different circumstances. Powers (1973; 2005) proposes that humans have 11 different levels of perceptual organisation that are created and organised through the normal life-cycle periods of development and growth. Many of these stages of development have been documented in studies of human infants (Plooij and van de Rijt-Plooij 1990). However, according to Powers, it is not what we call the levels which is important, nor how many of them there are; but rather, it is the way they function which is paramount.

Powers' (1973; 2005) proposal is that control at one level is established by varying the reference signal it sends to lower levels. It doesn't so much tell a lower-level system what to do; but tells it how close things are to the just right state. Also, perceptions at any particular level are combinations of inputs to that level from lower levels. This just means that abstract perceptions like 'kindness' are built from the ground up by combining more simple perceptions, such as 'comforting other people', which in turn is derived from more concrete experiences, such as 'using a soft voice'. Even more mundane concepts such as 'lasagne' are hierarchical in that a lasagne is derived from lower-level perceptions of the basic constituents of pasta, tomato, and cheese. For people, lower levels of a heirarchy consist of functions that involve specific processes and actions such as behaviours and actual muscle movements. Higher levels tend to relate to individual values and principles that include internal standards about how they might want themselves, the world, or other people to be. So, using the same example of 'kindness', wanting to 'be a kind person' would be an example of a higher-level internal standard, and below this goal would be lower levels representing exactly how one would achieve being a kind person, such as being considerate to others, offering to do things for people – right down to the lowest level of moving muscles to actually complete the task for that person.

'How?' and 'Why?' questions are useful ways of providing a sense of the differences between different levels. It is proposed that 'How?' questions help to shift a person's awareness down to lower levels whereas 'Why?' questions shift a person's awareness up to higher levels. If we were to ask you why you bought this book, you might say 'to learn about a transdiagnostic approach to CBT'. We could then ask 'Why do you want to learn about such an approach? to which you might answer 'So I can become a better clinician?' And if we asked 'Why do you want to become a better clinician?' you might say 'Because I like helping people'. We might then ask 'Why do you like helping people?' and you might reply with 'Because it's what I can do to make the world a nicer place'. From this simple example you might be able to appreciate the way in which 'Why?' questions help a person think about more important and more abstract goals.

To follow this example back 'down the staircase' we could start with 'How can you help to make the world a nicer place?' and one answer would be 'By helping people'. Notice already, that when answering a 'How?' question, there can be more than one possibility. And if we asked 'How can you go about helping people?' you might say 'By becoming a better clinician'. We could then ask 'How can you become a better clinician?' and you might reply with 'By learning about an approach to using CBT transdiagnostically'. Finally, we could ask 'How can you learn about an approach to using CBT transdiagnostically?' and you might say 'By buying this book'.

Obviously, the same line of questioning would lead to different places with different people. There is no right or wrong answer that is being sought – just exploration. Exploration can help a person become aware of what might have been there in their mind all along but they simply had not ever paid attention to it before.

While the idea of a hierarchy of internal organisation is not new, the distinctiveness of the PCT hierarchy arises through the detailed description of how the hierarchy actually functions. Knowing that goals at any particular level are being set by control systems at a higher level has important and direct clinical implications that will be explained in subsequent chapters. The articulation of ways in which awareness can shift up and down the levels through the use of 'Why?' and 'How?' questions is distinctive and provides essential knowledge for clinical practice.

Conflict

One aspect of mental health problems that tends to be dealt with only implicitly in current models, formulations, and questionnaires concerns the manifestation of psychological distress. There seems to be an unstated assumption that the items that are described on questionnaires are inherently distressing, for example, the notion that hearing voices must be, in and of itself, distressing. Our contention, however, is that for any distressing symptom of a mental health disorder, it is possible to find someone in the general population who also has that symptom but is *not* distressed by it. Some people hear voices but are not distressed by them. Some people prefer to avoid the company and scrutiny of others but that doesn't bother them. Some people have complex routines and habits and are not distressed by these.

We suggest, therefore, that symptoms of mental health disorders are not intrinsically distressing. This is not typically recognised in many questionnaires. A large collection of questionnaires can be found that ask about various symptoms, such as how often a person felt that everything was an effort, how often they thought life was meaningless, or how often they thought other people were evaluating them negatively. What is much more difficult to find, however, are any questions that ask people if they were *bothered* by these symptoms. One person might think life is meaningless and be distressed and upset about this whereas another person might think life is meaningless and peacefully accept this as the natural order of the universe. If people were to ask 'What is distressing about feeling paranoid?' (or depression or social phobia, or . . .), then we might get to the heart of the problem quicker.

It is not necessarily symptoms themselves that generate distress – but they are possible areas to investigate that might reveal some other underlying source of distress. From a control theory perspective, there is a principle of 'relativity', with regard to psychological distress, such that something is only ever a symptom of distress when it is considered relative to other thoughts, behaviours, or feelings. More specifically, symptoms of distress can be considered relative to an individual's personal goals. Someone will be distressed about the idea of a meaningless life if, simultaneously, they also want their life to be enriching and purposeful. Someone will be distressed about avoiding social contact if, simultaneously, they also crave the company of others. Distress arises therefore when a person is not able to realise their goals.

A common cause of distress, therefore, is when two incompatible goals are pursued simultaneously. Someone might want to pursue a rewarding career but also want to nurture warm and close family relationships. Someone might want to make their own decisions but also want the approval of a loved one. Whenever there is chronic psychological distress there is likely to be two incompatible goals doing battle with each other. Subsequently, neither goal gets realised!

The recognition of this type of conflict is widespread both generally and in clinical settings more specifically. Many of our everyday expressions and colloquialisms reflect conflict: being stuck between a rock and a hard place, a double-edged sword, having your cake and eating it too, caught between the devil and the deep blue sea, and biting the hand that feeds you are examples of the many ways we express conflict. Being in two minds, being in a dilemma, 'to-ing and fro-ing', being indecisive, unable to make up your mind, fighting with yourself and switching between alternatives are other examples of this internal conflict.

Many current approaches to therapy also recognise the importance of conflict. Motivational Interviewing describes an ambivalence in which people are in conflict about particular behaviours such as using alcohol and drugs (Rollnick and Miller 1995), Acceptance and Commitment Therapy (ACT) describes people waging a war against themselves (Hayes *et al.* 1996), Stiles' Assimilation Model suggests we have voices arguing with each other (Stiles *et al.* 2008) and Wells'

Metacognitive Model discusses people being 'in two minds' about worry (Wells 2000). Conflict is referred to, therefore, in various approaches. However, the centrality of conflict to understanding and treating psychological distress does not seem to have been fully appreciated.

From a control theory perspective, conflict involves at least three layers of the hierarchy of control systems (see Figure 8.1). At an upper level, signals are sent to the next level down that result in incompatible goals being set. For example, someone may try to be a good person by being both nice to other people and expressing one's own feelings. These goals would conflict when the situation involves having to be honest to a friend about something upsetting they have done. The person is stuck for words and indecisive, not knowing how to manage the situation. The mid-level of conflicted goals therefore sends signals to the level below that would then vacillate and vary unpredictably. Conflict, then, involves the level of symptoms at the bottom, the level of incompatible goals in the middle and the level that sets the conflict in motion at the layer above. Resolution of the conflict will occur when this highest level alters the signals it is sending downwards.

Carey (2008) describes some clinical examples that reflect the three-level model of conflict. For example, one client described the dilemma she found herself in as a parent. She wanted to let her daughter do normal things but she also wanted to keep her safe and not let her out of the house. These conflicted goals were generating anxiety, fear, and irritability. Above the conflicted goals seemed to be a system concerned with being a good parent (see Figure 8.2). Another client described feeling like a 'freak' that had horrific thoughts and images in her head. The client reported not wanting to be a freak and had multiple problems that had been summarised through labels such as Social Phobia and Borderline Personality Disorder. The client, however, also recognised that, in some ways, she liked being a 'freak'. There was a sense in which she could see the funny side to being a 'freak' and there were also some positive aspects to not being 'normal'. Therefore, above her struggle of being a 'freak' seemed to be a system controlling self-identity.

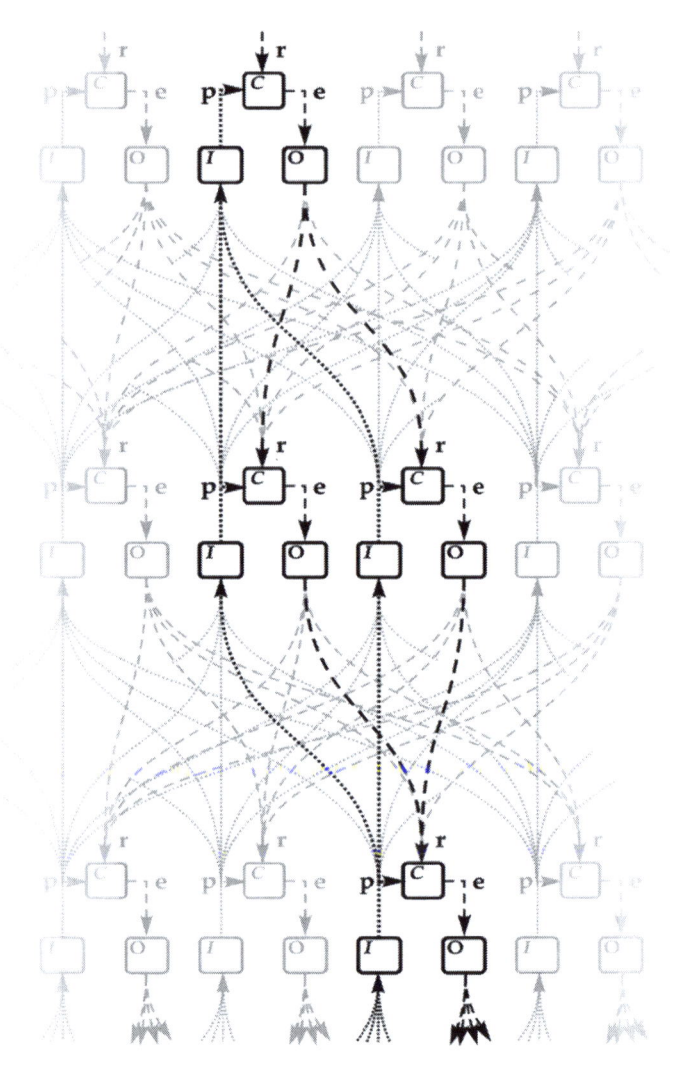

Figure 8.1 A PCT model of internal conflict. Reproduced with permission from *The Method of Levels: How to do psychotherapy without getting in the way* Timothy A. Carey, www.livingcontrolsystems.com.

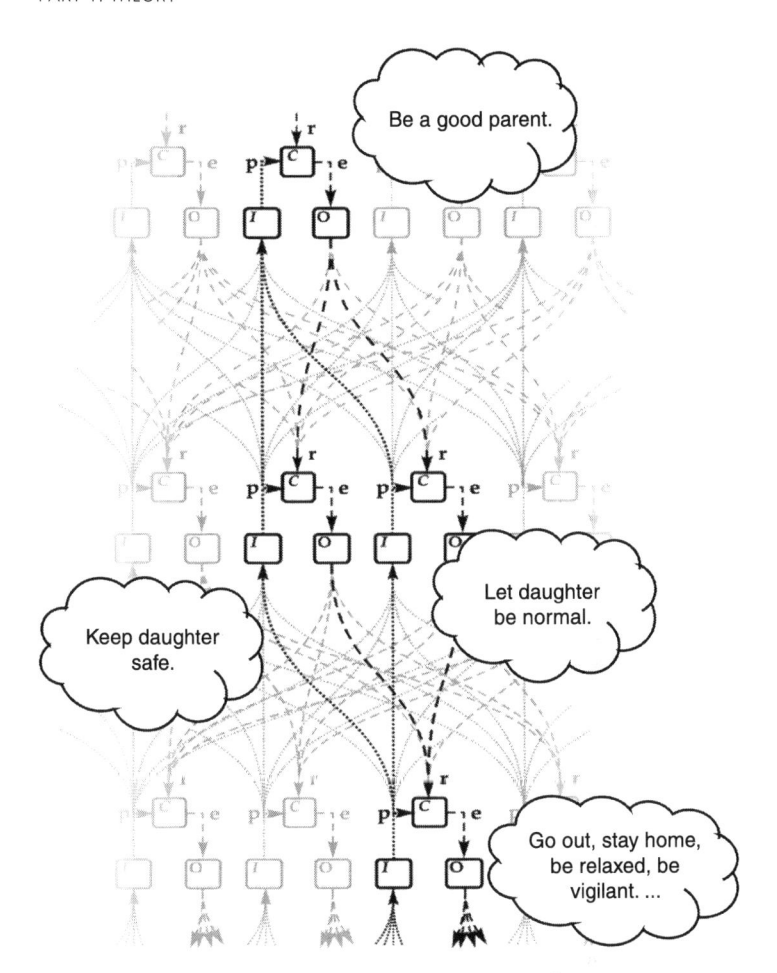

Figure 8.2 Conflict model with the clinical example of parenting mapped onto it.

An interesting feature of conflict is that the systems in conflict are not broken or sick or dysfunctional. In fact, it is quite the reverse. The better the control systems are, the more intense the conflict is likely to be. As one control system attempts to correct its error it increases the error for the other control system. Both systems then are attempting to minimise their own error but, in doing so, are increasing the error for the other system. Eventually the outputs of both systems reach their extremes and the systems are unable to effectively control. A debilitating feature of extreme conflict, therefore, is that it effectively disables two control systems within the person's repertoire. Clinical examples of the skilled ways that people may create conflict for themselves, through a highly developed process, include perfectionism, worrying, and acute awareness of physical complaints, for example.

The concept of conflict can help to explain some current phenomena in the field of psychological treatments. For example, people who are trying extremely hard to overcome an addiction will often have a dramatic 'relapse' where they re-engage in their addictive behaviour. This occurs because the goal of 'use alcohol to cope with my problems' does not disappear while the person stops drinking but is suppressed for a period of time until the relapse tips the balance back in favour of the suppressed goal. This kind of rebound effect is common and predictable within a model of conflicted control systems. Familiarity with the model of conflict, therefore, would improve relapse prevention programs as it would help therapists to guide people's attention to the deeper goals behind their addiction problem. People's reluctance to engage in therapy can often indicate conflict as well.

Psychological distress, therefore, arises from internal conflict. The conflict experience will vary from individual to individual but will have an underlying common form. Resolution of the conflict will also vary in the solutions that are generated and the time taken to do this, even though the process of resolution will be the same.

PART 1: THEORY

9

Reorganisation: a non-linear process of change

By the time we become adults we have often learned many effective ways of solving problems. Useful strategies abound that help people generate new alternatives or select the most appropriate option from a range of possibilities. Techniques such as 'brainstorming' and 'cost-benefit analysis' can help people develop better awareness of situations so they can see them more clearly and figure out appropriate solutions.

Solving problems and finding ways to change is fundamental to effective psychological functioning. Thus, it is also a central part of psychological treatment, yet plausible models of change are neither abundant nor easy to find in the profusion of psychological theories that are available. The delivery of most psychological treatments implies that a linear model of change is assumed to be the order of the day. Treatment is usually provided in regularly planned sessions that are booked in advance as though the way in which a person will resolve psychological distress can be predicted in a straightforward manner. Any sudden change that occurs, or a change that occurs early in treatment, is regarded as anomalous and possibly only superficial.

Despite the popularity of working according to a neat design of the change process, a linear model of change does not seem to accurately reflect the way change often occurs in nature. Adele Hayes and her colleagues (2007) make the point that change in many systems of nature is characterised by turbulence and instability, with growth and development often occurring suddenly and dramatically.

A model of change is needed, therefore, that can produce a variety of effects, including sudden and lasting change. Moreover, the change that is required for the resolution of psychological distress needs to be the type of strategy that can resolve intractable problems. For many of the dilemmas from which psychological distress springs, there is no existing solution. There is no way, for example, to simultaneously keep people happy and speak your mind. What is needed is a change mechanism that can generate novel solutions.

In the 1950s, while developing PCT, Powers was faced with many of these difficulties when he wanted to develop a plausible account of the way in which control systems were configured and compiled. The learning strategy required here needed to be so fundamental that it did not itself need to be learned. Powers developed a functional model that could successfully regain control through a random process of trial and error, and this has been tested in computer demonstrations (Powers 1973; 2005, 2008). Powers called the model 'reorganisation'. The fundamental idea is that when there is chronic loss of control (error) in the system, the reorganising mechanism begins generating random changes in the system. If the changes have the effect of reducing the error then those change strategies persist until the error increases again. If the changes do not reduce the error, another random change is generated.

This random trial-and-error process, therefore, has the qualities that are required. It is a fundamental strategy that does not need to be learned. Because it is random it can generate changes within a very short time period as well as over a long time frame.

The reorganising system has no sense of right or wrong or good or bad. It only seeks error reduction. It will not, therefore, necessarily come up with the best solution first. It will, however, continue generating changes for as long as the organism survives in order to reduce error in the system. In other words, we are all reorganising all of the time.

This robust and elegant system has important clinical implications. It suggests, for example, that change can happen suddenly and still be thorough and lasting. It also suggests that the best solution will not necessarily come along first. In fact, as reorganisation begins, the person might even feel that the situation is getting worse rather than better. Actually, sometimes a slight deterioration or increase in confusion, uncertainty, or emotionality can indicate that reorganisation has begun working. It is important to remain alert to ineffective therapy but it is equally as important to continue to promote reorganisation as it produces its effects. Advising clients ahead of time about what to expect can be a useful way of preparing them and providing them with information to help them persist in difficult times. We have provided an example of an information sheet about MDL we have used in clinical practice (see Appendix 3). It is also worth remembering that reorganisation might not necessarily occur during the therapy session where it is evident to the therapist. Reorganisation follows awareness. The aim of therapy is to facilitate the shifting of awareness so that the client can gain new perspectives created by reorganisation.

The reorganising system provides an optimistic attitude for the clinician. Change could, quite literally, be just around the corner. We do not have to see change as a long, slow process where increments are made gradually over an excruciatingly protracted period. Some change is like that, but crucially, the change process doesn't *have* to be like that. In fact, nothing in the activity of neurons happens over long time frames and psychological distress can manifest after just one distressing event. If distress can arise so quickly why should we not expect that it could also disappear as quickly? For some people lasting change can occur overnight. Why not set that as your goal and aim for that with all clients?

Reorganisation also gives us a new perspective for understanding common symptoms of psychopathology. Powers, for example, has suggested that there is an optimum range within which reorganisation works best. If reorganisation generates changes too slowly then the client might not able to reduce error before they are likely to give up and be depressed and immobilised. Is this, in fact, what severe depression is? On the other hand, if reorganisation occurs too rapidly, the client does not get the chance to experience the new change before another change is being generated. Could some experiences of psychosis be manifestations of changes and reorganisation that are much too speedy?

With the reorganisation process as a robust explanation of change, clinicians could begin to hope for much more in treatment. Fast effective change could be considered just as legitimate and just as possible as long slow change. Change according to the client's time frame could become the standard rather than an externally imposed expectation of how change will occur. Also, knowledge of the reorganisation process might help clinicians and their clients persist when things seem to be getting darker with the knowledge that a shiny new day might be just over the horizon. The reorganisation process does not know how to give up!

Awareness and imagination

Awareness could well be one of the most fascinating but least understood areas of human experience. The experience of awareness is undeniable, but what is awareness and, more importantly, what is it for? In this book we discuss one function for awareness that is suggested by PCT.

Perhaps the most interesting aspect of awareness is its mobility. At any time we can become aware of a wide range of experiences. As you read these words you might be aware of the letters on the page but you might also be thinking about a client you are currently seeing, or the jobs you will have to do once you have finished reading this, or the great movie you saw last night, or how comfortable the chair is that you are sitting in, or . . .

Awareness seems to move through our mind at will, highlighting various aspects of our lives to us. One analogy that has been used is standing in a large Gothic cathedral at midnight with just a flashlight. As you move the flashlight around, various parts of the cathedral become visible so you only ever see a small fraction of the cathedral at any point in time. It's important to keep in mind though that *all* the cathedral is still there *all* the time.

At any particular point in time we are only ever aware of a small fraction of the totality of who we are. The rest of who we are is still all there, however, it is just out of awareness – at least for this particular 'now'. This way of thinking about awareness provides some new insights for psychotherapy. For example, even though we have the experience of thoughts 'popping' into our heads, we might not be paying attention to them. What might actually be happening is that awareness has flitted over a different aspect of our hierarchy. Similarly, when we experience 'racing thoughts', it is actually our awareness that is racing – not the thoughts. As another example, when we have a song going over and over in our mind, it is awareness that is 'stuck' (at least while the song is playing) – not the song.

Given the mobility of awareness, it is puzzling to wonder what it is that moves it around. What is it that highlights the sound outside, or the implications of an idea you have just had, or the appointment you have tomorrow? One interesting aspect of awareness seems to be its automaticity. And one feature common to the things that are identified by awareness is a certain degree of 'error'. That is, we seem to notice the things that are not right, or perhaps the things that have the most amount of 'not rightness' at any particular moment. We also seem to notice areas in which some degree of emotionality occurs, but these could also be construed as signals to areas where there is the most 'not rightness' (or error).

It is important to remember that, from a control theory perspective, error does not mean 'bad' – it just means 'different from the expected or intended value'. If you have planned a dream holiday in six weeks' time, then imagining yourself in that dream destination will have error associated with it when you compare it with where you are right now. Control theory explains in some detail how we can manage to imagine our experiences and hold them in our mind's eye, as is often required in therapy. Essentially, the control hierarchy can short-circuit itself, half way down, to allow our stored images of a certain perception to be replayed as though happening in the moment; lower-level systems (e.g. talking) can continue in parallel. The technical details of this process are beyond the scope of this book (see Powers 1973; 2005) yet it is important to appreciate that an internal process of this kind can be modelled in a systematic way. It can also help to understand how unusual perceptual experiences within imagination, such as voices, impulses, and imagery, may ultimately be controlled more flexibly given the appropriate interventions, and therefore lead to less distress.

If awareness does move to the places where there is the greatest error at that moment, this might explain why people spend so much time thinking about their problems. The distress they are feeling is indicative of a large amount of error. As you question the client in detail about their problem, however, this seems to have the effect of briefly generating error in other systems. A meta-comment, for example, of 'That sounds crazy when I say it like that' might indicate some error between the way they want things to sound and the way things do sound as they are speaking. We will cover, in the Practice section, how Method of Levels therapy works on shifting awareness to facilitate change.

So, awareness seems to be attracted to error. That's useful to know from a therapeutic perspective because therapy deals with a lot of error. Another interesting aspect of awareness is that it seems to be intimately involved in problem resolution. It doesn't seem to be possible to change one's mind, or learn a new skill, or have an 'Aha!' moment without being aware of it. It may be for this reason that the general principle from a PCT perspective is that reorganisation follows awareness. So you can assume that wherever awareness is at any point in time, reorganisation is there too, tinkering away at improving control in that particular area. We will describe this in more detail in the next chapter but the implications for therapy are clear: awareness needs to be shifted to the source of the problem and kept there for long enough so that reorganisation can generate sufficient alternatives for a satisfactory solution to be found and control restored.

Arbitrary (or inflexible) control maintains distress via conflict

If chronic conflict leads to the loss of control, causing psychological distress and mental health problems, then what causes and maintains this conflict? That is where awareness comes in. Quite simply, it is the lack of awareness of the conflict, which in turn prevents reorganisation from making the necessary changes to reduce it. Within control theory, there is a particular term for how these elements can combine – arbitrary control. We have also used the term 'inflexible control' to describe the same process.

Arbitrary control is an attempt to control an experience (e.g. feelings, thinking, routines, other people) in a way that disregards the conflict that this attempt at control will create with other important goals (Powers 1973; 2005; Mansell 2005). This can occur between individuals or within individuals. A good example of when it takes place between people is trying to control another person for your own ends regardless of their wishes – coercion and manipulation are examples. There is significant evidence that 'overcontrolling', 'rejecting', or 'intrusive' parenting predicts adult mental distress (e.g. McLeod *et al.* 2007). Control theory proposes that each of these styles of parenting reflect arbitrary control whereby the parent is putting their own goals ahead of the legitimate needs of the child. We propose that, as children who have experienced this parenting style grow to be adults, by default, they tend to apply the same approach to their own feelings, thoughts, and other people. This looks different in different people, but can appear as emotion suppression, subjugating their own needs, self-criticism, worry, risk-seeking, indeed any of the diverse range of behaviours and thinking styles we reviewed in Chapter 2.

Arbitrary control is a familiar experience to many of us. In fact, any time it feels as though you're having to 'try too hard' to achieve something, or forcing yourself to do something, it is likely that the sense of effort is being generated by one or more other control systems of which you are currently not aware. In other words, there is some other goal that is causing conflict. There is another sort of 'trying hard' that occurs when, for example, someone tries hard in a tennis match or tries hard to beat their personal best time at 1500 m. This is not the same as arbitrary control. The 'trying hard' of arbitrary control is so effortful because there is another part of the person that wants the exact opposite from what they are trying to do. In effect, there is another part of you that is trying just as hard as the part you are aware of but this other part is hidden from awareness for the moment. For example, when someone 'tries hard' to be polite to someone they actually have little respect for; or someone 'tries hard' not to buy another packet of cigarettes when they really want another packet of cigarettes. In these situations, the sense of trying hard is because there is another control system that is operating away from awareness that, for some other entirely functional reason, wants the opposite goal of what is being pursued at the moment. When people talk about 'trying hard' in therapy, it is likely that there is a conflict lurking within and gains (reorganisation) will be made by helping the person become aware of a wider range of the things that are important to them, rather than continuing to perseverate on the single thing they are trying hardest to achieve. An example of arbitrary control can be provided with reference to a real client, 'Lisa'. She came to therapy reporting experiences of extreme anxiety, so bad at times that she found it difficult to get to work. She described her difficulties as being related to her sense of inability to reach her goal of being 'perfect', especially at work. She described her extreme efforts of trying to be perfect, by preparing for meetings and presentations at work until the early hours of the morning. During therapy, she became aware that the amount of time she invested in achieving this goal was causing her to miss out on spending time with friends and family, compromising her potential of achieving another important goal of meeting a partner and having her own family. Later, in the practice section of this book, we provide some examples of the MOL therapy Lisa received.

So, arbitrary control is therefore an attempt to reach a specific goal but in a way that has unhelpful consequences for many other goals that are at least equally important. In reality, all of us can apply arbitrary control to some things in our lives because there is a limited time to become aware of all the possible conflicts we might cause for ourselves. For example, we might try not to get upset in front of work colleagues but in doing so not be able to elicit their support. However, when this tendency is long lasting and applied in certain ways, it can be very damaging. For example, people who try not to feel certain emotions fail to benefit from where these emotions are useful to them – suppressing anger can conflict with the need for assertiveness; suppressing fear can conflict with the effective judgement of real dangers. People do not set out to use arbitrary control intentionally, but do so due to their lack of awareness of the negative, unintended consequences. Proneness to certain thinking styles can also make arbitrary control more likely. For example, people who are described as 'impulsive' may act very quickly and not consider at that moment the impact of their actions on their other goals. Conversely, people who are described as 'compulsive' may focus their attention for long periods on their immediate concerns (e.g. to remove an obsessive thought) without broadening their attention to other important goals in their life. Even more damaging are forms of arbitrary control that can be harmful to one's self-concept (e.g. self-criticism) or to oneself (e.g. self-harm and suicide). The challenge of addressing arbitrary control is not merely its inflexibility and severity. Often our clients perceive that they gain great advantages from these strategies and may have relied upon them to achieve important personal goals, even though they undermine other personal goals at the same time. A key example here is perfectionism (as in the case example of Lisa), which can generate advantages in terms of success in the working world, and yet is often associated with self-criticism and extreme efforts that damage self-esteem and relationships.

We shall see that effective therapy therefore involves raising awareness within the present moment of these processes and, in turn,

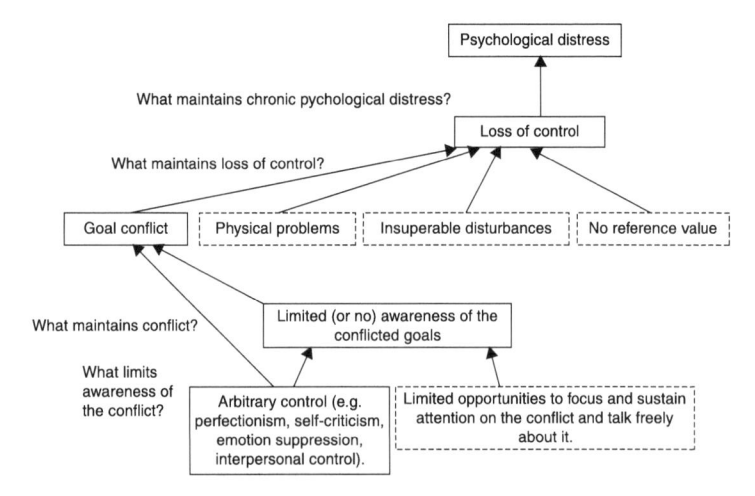

Figure 11.1 A diagram to illustrate how arbitrary control maintains goal conflict, which in turn contributes to chronic loss of control and psychological distress, alongside other factors covered in the book.

their capacity for both coping and distress. When people become aware of these broader perspectives and longer-term goals for themselves, they become more able to generate alternative ways of trying to control.

Figure 11.1 illustrates how arbitrary control maintains the loss of control involved in psychological distress via its effect on blocking important personal goals. In this diagram, the other contributions to loss of control, covered in Chapter 6, are illustrated as well.

PART 1: THEORY

12

Directing awareness to regain flexible control: a common factor of CBT, effective therapy and natural recovery

The principles we have been building up so far create an interesting implication for the mechanisms of effective therapy. We have proposed that psychological distress results from chronic loss of control caused by conflict. This occurs when people consistently try to control their experiences without being fully aware of the impact on other longer-term, and higher-level, goals. Thus, recovery involves regaining control at a more fundamental level. This is done through noticing how one is trying to control an experience at a given time, and allowing one's awareness to go 'upward' to consider how present moment actions have implications for long-term goals. When control is implemented by higher-level goals, it is more flexible and there is a wider range of different means to achieve the same end. This stands in contrast to trying to persevere with more concrete lower-level goals (e.g. to count to ten in one's head; to restrict one's eating; to punch a pillow) in the absence of considering the impact trying to achieve these goals is having.

There is good reason to believe that the core mechanism of any effective therapy is the degree to which it can help a person focus on a present moment perception in order to develop awareness of the associated higher-level goals (representing core personal concepts and principles), and the methods they are utilising to try and achieve control of these. This process is all in the service of regaining flexible control, which leads to natural recovery.

It appears that all active therapies involve tools for focusing awareness on present experience for longer than would otherwise occur (Carey 2011b). Behaviour therapies utilise systematic

53

exposure to feared stimuli, and cognitive therapies use thought catching and behavioural experiments to engage with current experiences. Mindfulness and acceptance therapies emphasise noticing and monitoring internal experiences in the present moment. Metacognitive approaches encourage focus on external perceptions but share the emphasis on the present moment. Historically, psychoanalysis capitalises on the current experience of transference and countertransference in the session, and person-centred counselling revolves around helping the client to describe their current phenomenological experiences.

Remarkably, a wide range of therapeutic approaches propose that it is also critical to bring the contents of higher-level systems into awareness. Theories diverge as to whether these systems are termed 'schemata' (Beck 1967), 'internal working models' (Bowlby 1969), 'metacognitive beliefs' (Wells 2000), 'personal constructs' (Kelly 1955), 'unconscious motives' (Freud 1930), or 'values' (Hayes *et al.* 1996). Yet, in each case they represent deeper concepts that are often outside awareness and whose effects unfold over the long term. Detailed interviews reveal that the natural recovery process also involves shifts at this deeper level (Carey *et al.* 2007; Higginson and Mansell 2008; Gianakis and Carey 2011). The people in these studies reported changing or developing their self-identity, becoming a more compassionate person, and changing the way they see the world.

It is the premise of PCT that the dynamic structure of these processes as forms of control is more important than their labels, and this structure is described in precise detail by PCT. Therefore, we should aim for the most parsimonious and efficient way to enable control in our clients. Method of Levels therapy is a transdiagnostic cognitive therapy based on the principles of PCT and is designed to achieve just that, through distilling the active ingredient of change within all effective therapies and natural recovery.

PART 1: THEORY

13

Interpersonal control

We have described how life involves the control of experience. We have also explained that control is normally carried out automatically and outside awareness. We only tend to notice when control is not working – often because of conflict.

The most common instance for creating conflict is when we try to control another person, or when we experience them trying to control us. Indeed, this is often the first sense of the term 'control' that comes to mind when we think of 'control freaks' and people who are 'controlling'. In actual fact, these may be the instances where control is not working well at all – as evidenced by the upset that people experience in their company.

It may not be a coincidence that CBT is grounded on the premise of the 'collaborative relationship', within which the therapist and client aim to work with, rather than against one another, for a shared goal – the client's well-being. There is little explanation in CBT itself of why a collaborative relationship is necessary. We can use control theory to elucidate this question.

There is a consensus that the origins of adult psychological distress across a wide range of disorders lie in experiences during childhood. These experiences are characterised by the basic needs of the child either not being met, through neglect, or being suppressed or controlled by powerful others (McLeod *et al.* 2007). Thus, our clients have had a history of being around people who put their own needs ahead of our clients'. Therapy needs to be about putting the client's needs first, and the techniques of the therapy introduced in such a way that this basic stance is not disturbed.

According to control theory, when we try to control another person, this is a form of arbitrary control and it is typically counterproductive. This is because a person has their own goals and, therefore, if what you try to control matters to that person, they will experience conflict with their own goals. An example would be if a parent shouts at their child for crying when the child is in pain. In the short term, this conflict might be met with counter-control as the child attempts to re-establish control, by shouting back for example, and thus tries to reduce the effectiveness of the parent's attempts at stopping them cry. This rarely works in a relationship with an individual who has power and on whom one depends. Therefore, in the long term, the child may learn that their goal for keeping the protection of their parents is more important than the goal of seeking comfort when in pain and so simply accept that shouting is a way of suppressing crying when in pain. The child's need for help when in pain is therefore not met and the child would continue to experience conflict when in pain in the future. This habit of mind would continue into adulthood.

According to this view, we need to be sensitive to interpersonal control occurring in therapy. Moreover, as we shall elaborate on in the next section, control theory provides a theoretical tool to try to understand when and how misbalances in collaboration can occur, and how to repair them.

PART 1: THEORY

Circular causality and model building

As clinicians, we often seek to identify the important factors that are responsible for producing the problems our clients are currently experiencing. Many of our existing models of psychological difficulties reflect this kind of straightforward linear approach, as do our methods of formulation. It is common, for example, to identify 'triggers' of particular episodes. Furthermore, part of our purpose in collecting information at the beginning of treatment is to suggest plausible hypotheses about critical events or periods that generated the 'biased cognitions'.

Implicit in our current CBT models is the idea that an outside event or internal dispositions cause particular behaviours. The models that are used in PCT, however, are different from existing models in general psychology. The basic principles of PCT are expressed in functional models rather than statistical or conceptual models (e.g. Powers 2008). Functional models are more rigorous than other models. They are often models about more fundamental behaviour and they are more specific than nonfunctional models. In many ways, it is not possible to compare functional and nonfunctional models: they just do different things. A child's drawing of a house and an architect's floor plan of a house could both be considered models of houses but they are useful for different purposes. As a piece of art to hang on the wall, the child's drawing is probably most suitable. For a blueprint of a way in which to construct the wall that the art might hang on, however, the architect's handiwork is likely to be the preferred model.

The choice of models to base one's psychological practice on may well be influenced by similar considerations. A functional model is more accurate and robust than a nonfunctional model but whether accuracy and robustness are important considerations is a matter for each clinician to decide. Functional models can also help with definitional problems because the terminology used in functional models is more precise than in nonfunctional models (Carey 2011b). In conventional psychology, for example, it can be very hard to define even something as simple as a 'stimulus' because of the conundrum that arises when something sometimes acts as a stimulus but at other times does not. The same reasoning applies to 'triggers'. Why are some things 'triggers' for some people but not for others or 'triggers' in some situations but not in others?

These difficulties are addressed within functional models where the important relationships are expressed in precise quantitative terms. For example, some people are bothered by the use of the term 'error' (e) to refer to the difference between the reference (r: a standard or goal) and the perception (p: a representation of a current experience). In PCT, however, as long as it is clear that what is being referred to is the difference between the reference and the perception then someone could use a term they felt more comfortable with. It is the relationship ($e = r - p$), not the word label that is important.

By building functional models, Powers (e.g. 2008) made some startling discoveries. One of these discoveries we have already described – that of behaviour controlling perceptions. Another of the central discoveries Powers made was that living things do not operate according to linear laws of cause and effect. For living things, circular causality is the order of the day. This means, to understand behaviour at any point in time, both the current goal and the current state of the environment need to be known.

Circular causality can be a difficult fit when one is used to thinking in terms of starts and stops and causes and effects. The real message behind circular causality is that there is always something going on prior to the cause and always something happening after the effect. Even the simple eye-blink reflex can demonstrate this point. The eye-blink reflex is used in many studies investigating learning processes. The basic approach is that a puff of air is directed towards the eye and a blink is recorded soon after. Variations can be introduced, such as sounding a little chime before the puff of air, to see if the timing of the blink varies. The devil, however, is in the details. The eye, for example, has to be in a particular state in order for the experiment to work – dead eyes will not be of any use in this experiment. Also, the puff of air needs to be directed towards the eye. A puff of air behind the back of the head will not be of any use in producing a blink.

Why are these things so crucial? Well, it turns out that the surface of the eye is in a particular state (maintained in that state by a reference that specifies a certain moisture level) and the puff of air disturbs that state. The blink? Well, the blink restores the surface of the eye to the pre-puffed state. So where we demarcate 'cause' and 'effect' is very much an arbitrary process. Is the puff of air a cause? Well yes, but what exactly does it cause? It causes the moisture on the surface of the eye to change. Is the blink an effect? Well yes, but it is an effect of a change in the moisture level on the surface of the eye. Is the blink also a cause? Certainly. The blink causes the moisture level to return to its pre-puffed state.

This might all seem a long way from psychological treatments and the resolution of psychological distress but it's not really that far. We are suggesting that psychological distress arises through disruption of the process of control, which is characterised by perception, comparison, and action. From the perspective of circular causality we could get used to saying these three things in any order: comparison, perception, action; action, perception, comparison, and so on. If some of those orders sound a bit strange, that might indicate how used to thinking in a linear fashion we are. These three processes are occurring constantly and simultaneously for as long we continue to breathe in and out.

For psychological problems, therefore, we do not need to spend time searching for apparent causes and triggers. How the problem got there is not so important. What is of much greater significance is what's keeping the problem there. And the process of problem maintenance is occurring in a dynamic and ongoing way. Understanding control and the process of reorganisation will help us move away from thinking about causes and effects to recognising satisfying day-to-day living as a process of specifying, creating and maintaining particular states (Bourbon 1995) in an ongoing and seamless way.

15

It's all perception

We have covered many principles in Part 1. Each of them builds on an idea about life, humans, and society that is unique, integrated, and sets the foundations for interventions based on control theory. How might we want to sum them all up?

'It's all perception.'

We know there is a physical world out there that obeys physical laws, but all we have, all we will ever have, is our perception of that world.

We know we can act on the world and behave in a vast variety of ways, but all we have (and all we will ever have) is our perception of that behaviour – for example through vision as we see ourselves in action, or through proprioception as we feel the location of our limbs and joints. We do not have a perception of the nerve signals that are sent towards the muscles, or any exact measure of the amount that a muscle is contracting – only our perception of that contraction from the senses that lie within our body.

This is the PCT view, that when we imagine, prepare, or enact a behaviour, it is the perception of that behaviour and its effects that we are perceiving. There is no objective measure of the behaviour. Behavioural psychologists vary widely as to whether they classify a behaviour as a category of act (e.g. writing), a time over which the act occurs following a change in the environment (e.g. reaction time), or a muscular reaction (e.g. electromyography (EMG) measures). A PCT account would propose that there are as many ways to classify behaviour as there are levels of control in a hierarchy, and yet it is only at the lowest level in the hierarchy in PCT that neural signals actually interface with muscles and glands.

Therefore, while there are continuous cycles of perception, comparison, and action going on as we speak, listen, etc., the only aspect that is in our awareness is the perception; and it is the control over this that is critical. This principle guides the kinds of questioning that form the interventions we will describe – helping people to shift their awareness and focus their attention on the perceptions that matter to them, with the ultimate result that they will learn to control them better over time, through reorganisation. It is like the tennis coach who insists – 'focus on the ball not your arms'. This kind of stance helps the therapist to take a step back from thinking that the client's behaviour can be manipulated, or controlled, if only the right intervention were to be provided. It helps therapists see that problematic behaviours or distressing symptoms are not the objects to be 'fixed'. According to PCT, the change that is necessary is only possible from the inside, by the clients themselves, and only then via their shifts in awareness at various levels that accompany the learning of new skills and thinking styles through the process of reorganisation.

Part 2

PRACTICE

PART 2: PRACTICE

16

The setting conditions: a problem that the client is willing to talk about

CBT from a control theory approach is a process of facilitating people to be able to restore control in those parts of their lives where it is currently disrupted. For this reason, the therapy is fundamentally a 'voluntary' process with the client being in charge of the topic being discussed. Each time the client attends a session, the clinician begins by asking them what they would like to work on in the time available. The client then begins describing the area that they are currently struggling with.

A control theory approach tells us that if therapy is mandated to people, there are good scientific reasons that it may not work (see Chapter 12 on arbitrary control). There are people who have been directed by the courts to attend an anger management program or an alcohol program, for example, and while therapy can be very successful with problems of anger or alcohol abuse, the decision about whether or not to have treatment can only ever be made by the individual receiving treatment. That said, sometimes there can be other areas that the person might want to talk about. The person, for example, might not think that their anger is a problem but they might be interested in finding ways to avoid making court appearances. Or, they might be willing to talk about the fact that they did not really want to attend, but did so anyway. This approach can work particularly well with adolescents who have, perhaps, been 'sent' to therapy by their parents for behaviour that the parent finds problematic. It may be that the adolescent does not agree with the parent's evaluation of the situation and doesn't see a problem with their behaviour. They may, however, be interested in getting their parents 'off their back' and a discussion around this topic might be useful. Ultimately though, if a client does not have something they would consider

65

talking about, there is really very little the therapist can do except leave an open invitation for the client to come back when they do have something they wish to speak about.

A control theory approach to CBT, therefore, has a different approach to issues such as engagement and insight. It is considered that the most engaging thing that can be done is to communicate respect and optimism to the client and to provide them with an experience of the therapy. If the person is reluctant or ambivalent about discussing their problem then this reluctance could be respectfully explored but the therapist would communicate to the client that they respect their decision not to engage in therapy. The therapist conveys by their manner and deeds that they believe the client is a capable, competent person who knows what they need to help their situation. That is not to say that, sometimes, giving clients information about the therapy, and what is involved, is not helpful. That sort of information might be extremely helpful to clients, but the ultimate decision about what to do with that information is theirs.

When considering insight, the person knows their own situation better than people around him or her. It is certainly the case that, sometimes, people appear to minimise problems or have very different accounts of their problem than that of those who are close to them. In these situations, it is important to remember the principle of behaviour controlling perceptions. The words people use are behaviours too. People use words to create particular perceptual effects. Concepts such as minimisation, denial, and insight can be considered differently from a control of perception perspective. When a person 'denies' they have a drinking problem, what effect does saying those words to you have for them? Our therapists do not spend any time convincing people that some area of their life is a problem if the person themselves does not think it is. When a person is reluctant to discuss their problems at all, what might that be achieving for them?

Sometimes people will begin a session by answering the 'What would you like to work on today?' question with 'I don't know'. This is quite an extraordinary response when you think about it. Imagine someone going to the trouble of making an appointment to see a dentist, getting themselves to the dentist's office, sitting in the dentist's chair, and then, when the dentist says 'What would you like me to look at today?' saying 'I don't know'!

The 'I don't know' could be communicating a range of things. Perhaps the client has more than one problem and they do not know which one to talk about first. Perhaps they do not know whether they made the right decision to come. Perhaps they are worried about how their problem might sound when they say it out loud. Perhaps things have improved since they made the appointment but they didn't want to cancel it and now they don't know what to do.

Any of these ideas could be things to ask about. The bottom line in our therapy is, if you don't know – ask. So, in response to 'I don't know' the clinician might ask 'Are you wondering if you've made the right decision to come in today?' or 'Do you have a few things to talk about and you're not sure where to start? Is it something else?' Whatever the response, it could be that the client is uncertain about whether they want to talk about their problems today. Again, the clinician could ask if the client wants to talk about their uncertainty – 'Would it help if we spent some time exploring your uncertainty about whether you should be here or not?' The bottom line, however, is that if the client really does not want to discuss their problem then that decision should be respected. The clinician could say something like 'Well, I don't want to make you talk about things if you're not sure that you want to discuss them, so why don't we leave things for today and you can make another appointment the very next time you would like some help with exploring your difficulties'.

The therapy that is conducted with the client is one area of their life and an area within which it is important that they can exercise control. The clinician does as much as they can to promote this by following the client's lead in terms of the topic of conversation, and even whether or not the conversation proceeds.

PART 2: PRACTICE

The stance: to enable the client's flexible control as efficiently as possible

As we described in Part 1 – 'to live is to control'. It is through effective control that a sense of purpose is achieved and maintained. However, we also made it clear that any form of control is prone to conflict – trying to achieve one goal can interfere with another. Earlier we described how attempts at controlling a specific experience that don't take into account other goals are known as arbitrary control. Often our clients' arbitrary control can be deeply rooted because it serves important personal goals at the same time as undermining others. So, for example, the client who has learned to depend on other people to do things for them whenever they feel vulnerable or anxious may see the benefits of this in the continuation of their relationships with caring people. Yet, this attempt at control is incompatible with other important goals the person holds – to live an independent life and to travel alone when necessary. Therapy is designed to help people develop awareness of conflict between goals so they can find solutions. This might involve considering the benefits and drawbacks of any attempts at control in different situations.

Thus, the opposite of arbitrary control is a form of control that is flexible and adaptive because it takes account of the many goals a person holds, and it considers how they are related. Importantly, we cannot know simply by observing a behaviour whether it is arbitrary or flexible. This can only be defined when the person's other goals are known.

For example, the process of pushing traumatic memories to the back of one's mind is often regarded as 'dysfunctional'. A control theory approach would instead argue that this depends on the context of other goals and the individual's awareness of these.

An example of arbitrary control via memory suppression:

- Mary suppresses her memories of a train crash because they are experienced as upsetting.
- Mary wants to try to recover from the trauma and go back on the train to get to work.
- Whenever Mary starts to think about going to work, the memories make her upset and so she puts all her attention into pushing them to the back of her mind. Mary spends a period of time struggling with these memories rather than thinking about how to get to work.
- Mary does not manage to get back on the train to work.

In this example, while Mary suppresses her trauma memories, she is not thinking that she actually needs to think about the crash to work out how to be safe when she returns to rail travel. She is only aware of being upset, and so she puts all her efforts into pushing the memories to the back of her mind. In doing so, her goal of facing her fears and getting back to work is left for another day.

An example of flexible control via memory suppression:

- Mary suppresses her memories of a train crash because they are experienced as upsetting.
- Mary wants to try to recover from the trauma and go back on the train to get to work.
- Whenever Mary starts to think about going to work, the memories make her upset.
- Mary chooses to push the memories to the back of her mind if she is with her mother because her mother tells her to just 'pull herself together', which would make her feel even worse.
- Mary chooses to let the memories stay in her mind, even though she is upset, when she is in therapy, when she is by herself, or when she is with her partner because she feels safe enough in these situations. This helps her start to make sense of what happened.
- Mary eventually gets back on the train to work and realises she can cope with feeling upset.

In the second example, the same behaviour of memory suppression is used. However, now Mary herself takes control of when to use it and when not to use it, based on feedback from her own experiences of how well it works in different contexts. Within control theory, this would imply that Mary has 'gone up a level' because she can now vary her goal for how much, and when, to suppress trauma memories. The same behaviour is no longer arbitrary – it is now flexible, and driven to support her own long-term goals.

This stance towards behaviour is taken throughout any session that is guided by control theory. A behaviour is only a problem if it is incompatible with the realisation of other goals that are important to the client. Critically, it is the lack of awareness of the other incompatible goals driving behaviours which can make the client feel that those behaviours are 'uncontrollable'. The therapist's questions might explore this notion of uncontrollability of a behaviour in order to think about deeper, more important goals, rather than arbitrarily classing a certain behaviour as 'good' or 'bad'.

One of the reasons that arbitrary control occurs is that people are such complex beings, it is genuinely hard to control and balance everything that matters in one's life on a moment-by-moment basis!

Priorities are often driven by changes in a person's life. An attack by a stranger demands quick reactions. A disruptive family environment may require single-mindedness. A realisation of one's damaging effects on others may demand a period of self-criticism. These each involve being 'in control' for important reasons. A control theory approach explains why our minds prioritise these goals at certain times, and why, also, each of us needs regularly to engage in a more reflective, flexible mode, so that the conflict caused by these immediate and concrete goals can be regulated and ultimately, more valuable, long-term goals can be achieved. This applies to every one of us, not just people seeking therapy.

PART 2: PRACTICE

Method of Levels goal one: asking about the current problem

If people can be helped to develop new insights and novel perspectives about their current problem, the first thing that needs to happen is that they need to focus their attention on their problem. That's not too difficult for many clients. When clients seek out assistance they are usually spending quite a lot of time thinking about their problem. The therapist helps sustain this focus by asking the client questions about their problem.

Method of Levels (MOL) is the transdiagnostic CBT based on Perceptual Control Theory (PCT). Its origins lie in the 1950s, when Powers himself experimented with how questioning can help people describe the different levels of perception in PCT. Tim Carey liaised with Powers in the 1990s and 2000s to build this questioning into a trainable therapy for mental health problems (Carey 2006).

The first aim of MOL is to facilitate the client talking about the problem in an un-censored way so they can engage in exploration of their difficulties. The therapist's role in this is to ask questions that facilitate the client maintaining focus on the issue at hand. The questions need to be short, specific, and clear, and asked only one at a time. The questions asked in MOL are not being asked to guide or direct or persuade clients of any particular solution or viewpoint of the therapist. The questions are not even really being asked so that the therapist can understand the client's problem clearly (although that is often one of the outcomes of this type of questioning). The point of the questioning is so that the client can develop awareness of new perspectives to understand their problem differently than they do currently.

Given that the client has probably spoken about their problem to at least some other people before they come to talk to you as a therapist, the conversation with you needs to be different from the conversations they have had with other people. At least, it needs to be different if the outcome is going to be different (presumably they have not resolved their problem by talking to other people otherwise they wouldn't be talking to you – so if they are going to resolve their problem by talking with you, the conversation needs to be different from other conversations). The following dialogue was taken from an MOL therapy session with a client – 'Lisa'. It was the initial session with the client and demonstrates the way in which a session might begin and how questions can be used to help the client begin to talk about a problem.

Therapist: Hi Lisa. What would you like to spend time talking about today?

Lisa: Well, I'd like to talk about my nerves. I'm feeling really anxious at the minute and it seems to be getting a lot worse, which is why I think I might need some help.

Therapist: Ok, so 'nerves' and 'anxious' . . . you used both those terms. Are they similar?

Lisa: The same.

Therapist: The same? Ok. So, the nerves and anxiety thing has been getting worse . . . what, recently?

Lisa: Yes, it's been getting a lot worse.

Therapist: Ok, so when you say a lot, how much is a lot?

Lisa: I think it's doubled.

Therapist: Right.

Lisa: Well, I'm usually an anxious person anyway, but it's serious at the minute.

Therapist: Right, so the way it was before wasn't so serious?

Lisa: It was manageable.

Therapist: Right, ok. And now, when you say it's doubled . . . is it serious but still manageable?

Lisa: It's not manageable.

Therapist: Hmm. Does it bother you that it's not manageable?

Lisa: Yes, because I've had to come here and see you and I'm struggling to get to work.

PART 2: PRACTICE

Therapist: Can you tell me a bit more about that struggle?
Lisa: Urm . . . well I get up in the morning and it's hard to get ready for work because I'm a bit of a perfectionist, so it takes me a long time to get ready. Urm . . . *(client pauses and eyes tear up)*.
Therapist: What's going through your mind just now?
Lisa: Just that this is difficult to talk about.
Therapist: Can you talk about the difficulty?
Lisa: Umm . . . *(client takes deep breath and looks tearful)* . . . about my anxiety?
Therapist: Well, the difficulty in talking about it.
Lisa: Urm . . . well, I've not talked about it before *(client's voice starts to break as she becomes more tearful)*.
Therapist: Yes, and as you're talking about it now, what's happening for you?
Lisa: I'm feeling more anxious.
Therapist: Is that right?
Lisa: Uh-huh.
Therapist: So when you say more, is that the level it's been at? The unmanageable level?
Lisa: It's worse than this, a lot worse.
Therapist: So the way you're feeling now is a lot worse?
Lisa: Urm . . . when I'm at home and when I'm at work it's a lot worse than it is now.
Therapist: Ok.
Lisa: So, this is just an example of how I get really anxious.
Therapist: Sure, so when you say anxious, what is anxious for you? Can you describe it?
Lisa: It's trying to do everything perfectly . . . and there's not enough time in the day.
Therapist: To do everything perfectly?
Lisa: Yes.

MOL questions are asked with genuine curiosity in order to encourage enquiry and exploration where nothing is taken for granted. Any time you assume (even implicitly) that you know what the client is talking about, you will be inadvertently preventing them from exploring their problem in detail. So, assume nothing. That means nothing more complex than asking clients to elaborate on whatever it is they are telling you about. If a client begins by saying something like 'I've been really depressed lately' you might say, in the spirit of curiously promoting exploration, 'Tell me about being depressed' or even just 'Depressed?'

One way of encouraging the client's detailed exploration of their problem is to think quite literally and concretely about whatever it is the client is telling you. If the client says something like 'I just push it to the back of my mind' you might think this is an area worth exploring in more detail. Asking questions like:

- 'How far back do you push it?'
- 'Where is the back of your mind?'
- 'What else is at the back of your mind?'
- 'Is it at the back of your mind right now?'
- 'Tell me about the back of your mind.'
- 'What is it about the back of your mind that makes it the right place?' 'Does it ever go back there without being pushed?'
- 'What happens once you've pushed it back there?'
- 'How can you tell when it's at the back?'
- 'Are there other things you push to the back of your mind?'
- 'Do you vary how far back you push different things?'

In the above example, the sample questions highlight the emphasis on processes. That is, you can ask about the process of 'pushing' and also the content of 'the back of my mind'. Asking about process as well as thinking about things concretely and asking rather than assuming, can be useful principles to promote curious questioning. Following these principles should help therapists generate questions about 'how much', 'how often', 'how many', 'whereabouts', 'what then', and 'anything else'. All of these questions will help clients develop a familiarity with their problem that they previously may not have had.

During practice and supervision, we have seen that the first goal of MOL is vital even though it does not attempt to shift the client immediately to their 'higher-level' goals. Imagine you are exploring a house for the first time. You would want to look around a room to get a sense of its size, its contents and its entrances and exits, before rushing to explore the next room in the house. Stopping in each room and taking in each level of the house one at a time would help you to build up a clearer picture of the house so that it is easier to find your way around and see what delights or dangers are in each room. If you were to rush to find the top room in the building straight away, it might be harder to remember how to get back downstairs or locate other rooms that are essential (e.g. the kitchen and bathroom!). This metaphor has its parallels in the perceptual hierarchies we described in Part 1. Each level in a hierarchy contains a variety of goals and preferences and their perceptual detail. We want our clients to learn to navigate their own awareness through this hierarchy rather than to rely on the therapist, or to learn ways of thinking abstractly or intellectually without linking these higher-level thoughts to the 'foundations' of the systems below. We often notice that after exploring the present problem in detail for a while, our clients start to show their own indications of 'going up a level'. These are called 'disruptions' and we target them in the second goal of MOL.

PART 2: PRACTICE

Method of Levels goal two: asking about disruptions

It is necessary for the client to develop a more in-depth awareness of their problem but it is not sufficient that this is the only thing that they become more aware of. According to the control theory formulation of multi-level conflict generated distress, a person's problems involve at least three levels of their perceptual hierarchy. When people describe their problems, however, they are attending to only particular levels of their problem.

From a control theory perspective, the level at which a problem manifests is different from the level at which the problem is generated. Understandably, people are mostly aware of where the problem is manifesting. For the problem to be resolved, however, people need to become aware of the areas that are generating the problem.

We have already described the way in which we can experience thoughts or other internal experiences, such as images or feelings, differently. We can be aware of things that seem to be at the front of our mind and, while we're aware of these, we can also be aware of parallel thoughts that seem to 'pop' into our mind. These other thoughts that we are only fleetingly aware of can often be the key to solving the difficulty currently being discussed.

As clients are encouraged to discuss their problems therefore, through the use of curious questioning, they will often become briefly aware of things related to what they are talking about. These shifts in awareness are inferred from subtle and not so subtle changes in the client's behaviour as they speak. It is a common phenomenon that can be observed during friendly conversation as well as televised interviews with people like politicians and athletes that, as people speak, they often have 'disruptions' to their stream of dialogue.

MOL GOAL TWO: DISRUPTIONS

While people talk, their speech is often disrupted in various ways. These disruptions are so commonplace that they often go unnoticed by the listener. One of the things that an MOL therapist has to do, therefore, is become attuned to these disruptions.

As you curiously question the client (without assuming anything) about their problem, you might notice that, at different times, they pause, or look away, or smile to themselves, or become teary, or shake their head, or increase the volume or rate of their speech (or decrease either of these things), or make a comment such as 'that sounds ridiculous' or 'I just don't know anymore'. In MOL, it is assumed that these occurrences indicate a sudden shift of awareness. Often, but not always, these shifts will be to the higher level from which the problems are being generated. In the last chapter, we used an example of a real MOL therapy session with a client called Lisa, who identified her need to be perfect as causing her distress. Here is another excerpt from her therapy that provides an example of how asking about disruptions might look.

Therapist: So, when you say you try to do everything perfectly, are you trying to do something perfectly now as we're talking?

Lisa: Urmmm . . . *(client smiles)* . . . maybe.

Therapist: And . . . you're kind of smiling?

Lisa: Well, . . . *(client laughs)* . . . because I'm trying to sit well . . . and I don't want to cry because my makeup will run . . . and, you know, that goes against that I think I should always look and be perfect.

Therapist: Ok, and so at the moment, as we're talking, you are even sitting and talking perfectly, and wanting to look perfect?

Lisa: Yes.

Therapist: How are you going with that?

Lisa: It's, it's . . . *(client laughs)* . . . it's hard.

Therapist: So, what makes you laugh?

Lisa: Urm . . . well it's hard to be perfect . . . because no one's perfect.

Therapist:	No one?
Lisa:	*(Client pauses and gets tearful.)*
Therapist:	How do you feel about that?
Lisa:	Urmmm ... *(client becomes more tearful)* I don't know. I'm sorry ... I'm just getting upset here.
Therapist:	Are you ok to keep talking?
Lisa:	It's fine.
Therapist:	Are you sure?
Lisa:	Yes.
Therapist:	What are you mulling over just now?
Lisa:	I'm just thinking that I'm always trying to strive to be someone else, or to be better. I look at examples of other people, and think oh, if I could be like them ... or be like them ... But, at the same time, I'm thinking that they have flaws as well ... and perhaps they're not perfect.

The fundamental purpose of asking curious questions, therefore, is to find a way to shift awareness to these relevant higher levels. When a disruption occurs then, it is important to ask questions about the disruption. By asking questions, you are helping the client shift their awareness and focus on this other thought for a sustained period of time. Questions like the following help the client to keep their attention on whatever it was that caught their attention only briefly.

- 'What came into your mind when you paused just now?'
- 'What did you think to yourself just then?'
- 'What made you shake your head just now?'
- 'What is it that's making you smile?'
- 'You're frowning as you describe this to me.'
- 'I noticed your voice is getting louder as you're speaking about this.'
- 'When you say it sounds ridiculous, what are you referring to?'

Once these questions have been asked, following up with two or three other questions on this area will help keep the client's attention at this place for longer than it otherwise might have been.

Sometimes the sudden disruption and shift in awareness will not be to a place that is relevant to the problem. If your enquiry reveals that you have gone down a fruitless path then a simple redirection such as 'We seem to have got a bit off topic, we were talking about . . . ' will get things back on track. Also, if every disruption was questioned then the client would barely be able to describe their problem and it might even feel like an interrogation! For this reason some judgement is required concerning those disruptions about which to ask. It is hard to provide specific guidelines about this, but MOL therapists seem to become more discerning with experience. The judgement can vary from client to client and problem to problem. One useful principle may be that those disruptions that seem to have heightened emotion associated with them are likely to be particularly useful.

By helping to keep a client's awareness at levels above the level where the problem is manifesting, you will be doing as much as you can to position the reorganising process in the place where it can do the most good. Which is the right level? That is not something that our current knowledge would allow us to answer, but a useful guiding principle is that if the problem still exists, a higher level should be searched for. If there is a problem, think 'up a level'. From the perspective of reorganisation there might be nothing else that matters as much.

Using the past, controlling the present, and living for the future

In this section we attempt to crystallise the mindset that a Method of Levels therapist attempts to foster and sustain in their clients. The outcome of this mindset is that the client is able to control more *flexibly*, in contrast to some of the inflexible or arbitrary methods they may have been using. It is important to note that flexibility is *relative*. For example, a person might be flexible in the ways that they try to suppress their feelings of sadness (e.g. blocking thoughts, changing conversation topic, taking medication) but *inflexible* in how they use this way of controlling – for example it might be their only way of coping with grief or loss and therefore this style of coping will conflict with any goals they have about remembering, reminiscing, or celebrating the life of a deceased family member.

The relative nature of flexibility is another reason why MOL works by going 'up levels' of goals. We are helping clients to see that what might work in the short term might not work in the long term for higher level goals. In MOL, we facilitate this by asking people about the flexibility of what they are doing. For example:

- 'How much sadness is too much?'
- 'What is important about controlling these feelings for you?'
- 'Are you trying to control your feelings right now? How is that going?'
- 'If the feeling is there now, what are you doing with it?'

MOL is not really about getting a person to stop thinking one thing and replace it with a different thought, or to stop acting out a specific behaviour in favour of something that could be considered more 'adaptive'. This could be likened to trying to switch something 'on' or 'off'. Instead, in MOL, the process of developing more flexible control would be more suited to the analogy of using a dimmer switch or volume control. We facilitate the client exploring how much worry, for example, is enough and when it might be too much and interfere with other important personal goals being achieved. In previous chapters we have used the example of a client, 'Lisa', who struggles with wanting to be perfect at work and feels conflicted between the goals of working hard and spending time with friends. This section of therapy demonstrates how a typical exploration of control within MOL therapy might sound.

Therapist: Ok, so when you are out doing other stuff, you're thinking that you should be back working.
Lisa: Yes.
Therapist: And does it work the other way too? When you're working, do you ever think you should be socialising?
Lisa: No, never. If I miss out on someone's birthday or I know that there's a social event going on, perhaps I think I should be there . . . *(client pauses)* but . . .
Therapist: What made you stop just there?
Lisa: Because I can think of examples when I have been studying at home or in the office and felt guilty that I wasn't out for a friend's birthday.
Therapist: Hmm, right. So, sometimes you feel guilty at work if you're not . . .
Lisa: If I'm studying or working in the office late at night.
Therapist: You might feel guilty?
Lisa: Yes.
Therapist: And then if you're socialising, you feel like that's a waste of time and you should be working.
Lisa: Yes, that's right.
Therapist: Ok, and the guilty thing is more about working late?
Lisa: I feel guilty for my friends.
Therapist: Right.

PART 2: PRACTICE

Lisa: Because it's got to the stage where they stop asking me to go out to places because they know the answer is usually no.
Therapist: Because it's a waste of time?
Lisa: Well I don't tell them that. I make an excuse and say I've just got work.
Therapist: And is that when you start to feel a bit guilty?
Lisa: Yes.
Therapist: How are you feeling just now whilst we're talking about it?
Lisa: I feel ok, because it's good to talk about these things and see where the problem lies.
Therapist: Hmm. Are you kind of trying to see where the problem is whilst we're speaking?
Lisa: Yes.
Therapist: In what sense, Lisa?
Lisa: I'm just trying to think how I can get a better balance in life.

We have stated already that MOL focuses on the present moment – after all, this is where control is happening – right now. However, our clients will often bring up the past and they will often be worrying or planning about the future. Clearly, this is a normal tendency – none of us live in a bubble where only the present counts. In PCT this is fully accounted for. First, our memories of the past (e.g. the location of our homes) can be used as reference values for present action (Powers 1973; 2005). Second, our higher-level goals (e.g. to be worthwhile) are actually perceived over longer time scales than the lower-level goals, and so feedback for these goals is often dependent on events that unfold over time. In the therapy, this part of the theory can be summarised as 'using the past, controlling the present, and living for the future'. The phrase helps to confirm that the present is where control occurs, but that present moment is using, and often modifying, past experiences to guide goals that extend into the future. MOL is definitely not the idea of 'living in the moment' that some clients use as a way of coping in the short term – control occurs in the now of the present moment but life itself has many moments that extend a lot further back and forward than the now of the current conversation. PCT conceptualises life as a seamless, ongoing, continuous process of control and not a process of leap-frogging from one 'in the moment' experience to the next. Now is not a moment, it's a life!

It is important to note that 'controlling the present' can involve efforts to spot and let go of one's usual inflexible habits that cause awareness to shift away from the problem at hand. It is only in the present that we can choose what experience to control, and how to control it. For example, a client with worries about their health may be in the habit of either worrying extensively about the future, or trying to block these worries out of their mind when they get too distressing. Controlling present experiences in a flexible way would involve noticing the thoughts, feelings, and images that are experienced and making an informed choice about how to manage them. At times, this might involve putting worries to one side (e.g. when trying to concentrate at work) whereas at other times it may involve holding them in your mind and exploring them (e.g. when keeping a diary or trying to work out how to get the right help). It is our view that PCT provides the conceptual framework necessary to bring together a range of descriptions of this kind of mindset – variously termed 'decentring', 'mindful awareness', or 'broadening perspectives' – and explain why it is fruitful for people.

The stance described here can help to generate questions in MOL that validate the past and future but make it clear that it is being seen through the lens of right now, and has to be relevant to the present. From this contextual perspective, arbitrary control methods are viewed as functional as opposed to abnormal. Nonetheless, in the present moment, there are also other goals to consider and thus there is an emphasis on increasing flexibility of control methods, as opposed to just abandoning them altogether. When a client ruminates on their past failures or predicts future catastrophes, the MOL therapist is interested in the effects that ruminating or predicting is having right now for the client. It is important that clients feel some sense of control in the present, even though they are struggling hard to control their futures or make sense of their pasts. Otherwise they can experience overwhelming feelings of loss of control as their minds are drawn to unchangeable past events or future ones that are hard to predict.

As an example, when a client reports, 'I have just messed up. I just blame myself for him dying and that is all I think about,' we could attempt the following questions:

- 'What does "messed up" look like?'
- 'Are you blaming yourself right now? What happens when you do that?'
- 'Does it bother you that you blame yourself?'
- 'How much do you actually want to blame yourself?'
- 'What do you *want* to think about at the moment?'
- 'How are you feeling right now as you are telling me this?'
- 'Is it all you are thinking about at the moment, or is there anything else going on for you?'

In contrast, some clients spend their mental lives far in the future: 'I am terrified of losing him. I spend all day and night worrying about all these bad things that might happen.' In MOL, we might try:

- 'How terrified do you feel talking about this right now?'
- 'Are you imagining losing him at the moment? What's going on there for you?'
- 'How many bad things are you thinking about at the moment?'
- 'How much are you worrying now? What does worry involve for you?'
- 'How much would you want to worry about losing him?'
- 'How does it make you feel when you worry about losing him?'

You may notice that in none of these simple vignettes is the therapist discounting the past or the future – this content is legitimate and useful for the client. Yet, the questions bring the awareness that thinking about this really is in the present, and not in a virtual life that is away from the room sitting in front of the therapist. Ideally, these questions, whilst 'bringing reality to bear', also provide options and choices about how to think and manage things right now. Indeed, there appears to be a converging indication that the most successful interventions bring long-term goals, beliefs, and values into 'contact' with present moment experiences, feelings, and actions (Mansell 2011). Method of Levels is merely one way of doing this, but one that we feel is particularly succinct and neatly linked to a scientific theory.

PART 2: PRACTICE

21

'Green Apples': working through problems without disclosure

MOL is clearly focused on helping clients resolve the distress they are experiencing. To do this, a process of guided self-exploration is facilitated in which clients spend time examining their cognitive processes, including thoughts and images, in order to create new and more satisfying experiences for themselves. Because of the focus on the client's inner subjective world, a unique feature of MOL is that the clinician doesn't need to know what the topic of conversation is.

Not very often, but on occasion, it has been the case that a client has a particular trouble that they feel uncomfortable discussing. When this occurs, it is incredibly rewarding (not to mention useful) to explain to the client that a conversation can occur without them divulging the topic to the clinician. Rather than encouraging the client to disclose what they are bothered about, or discussing some other topic, an MOL conversation can occur without the clinician learning about the particular topic.

If the client has a topic they find difficult to talk about, they could call whatever is bothering them 'marmalade', or 'falling snow', or 'Trevor', or 'green apples' (or some other term of their choosing). The clinician can ask them questions about marmalade and notice disruptions and direct their attention to these without ever knowing what the 'real' problem is. In this instance the therapy proceeds as it normally would. In fact, in some ways it is easier to be curious about this topic because the clinician really does have no idea of what the client is talking. It is easy not to make assumptions when it is a topic of which you are unaware. This can be especially useful for clients where trust might be an issue early on; for example, someone experiencing voices or unusual beliefs where they do not feel comfortable describing them as such.

Often in this situation, the client will begin discussing their problem as 'falling snow' (or any other term they choose) but then, as the conversation proceeds they will feel more comfortable and let the clinician know what the topic is. Even if this doesn't happen though, MOL can still continue. In fact, an entire session can be conducted in this manner.

When the client first starts talking about 'green apples' the clinician can ask curious questions such as whether or not it bothers them to have green apples, how long have green apples been a problem, are there any times when green apples aren't troublesome, and so on. Questions can also focus on where the green apples are as the client talks about them. Are they right at the front of their mind, towards the back of their mind, or do they move around? Are there lots of them or just a few? Are there some places where they seem more problematic than others? Do they change as the client talks about them – do they fade in or out, do they get bigger? Are there any sounds, smells, or feelings associated with the green apples? If there are, similar questions can be asked about how these other sensations change as the person notices them.

As with other MOL sessions, the purpose of asking these curious questions is to promote the presence of disruptions. When disruptions occur, the clinician should ask about them as they normally would. The fundamental purpose of helping clients shift their awareness to levels above the experience of their distress remains unchanged. So when clients pause, or look away, or shake their head, or when their talking slows down or speeds up, the clinician can ask about what might be happening for the client.

- 'What made you pause just now?'
- 'You're shaking your head as we speak – is there something in your mind you're responding to?'
- 'I noticed as you talk you're slowing down what you're saying – is something occurring to you or something else grabbing your attention?'

The ability of MOL to work without the clinician even knowing the topic of conversation highlights some unique aspects of this type of transdiagnostic cognitive therapy. It is not important, for instance, to know whether or not the client is telling you the truth. The client's job is to work on whatever it is that is bothering them and the clinician's job is to help them do that by keeping them focused on the conversation. It would be of very little value for the client to be talking about something that was actually not what they were bothered about.

Similarly, it is not necessary for a clinician to collect large amounts of information in order to be able to put together a comprehensive 'picture' of how the client came to be troubled in the way that they are. It is definitely important to know about the client's risk of harming themselves or others, and it is still possible to establish this without knowing the exact problem the client is talking about. However, beyond that, the most important aspect to MOL is helping them examine their troubles as they currently experience them.

To get the wrinkles out of a shirt it needs to be ironed in the immediacy of the here and now and it doesn't really matter how the wrinkles got there. MOL is like ironing for the mind in which the current identified wrinkles are smoothed away leaving a fresh, crisp perspective that is ready once again to step out into the sunshine and embrace life.

What to say at the first session

Method of Levels is designed to be efficient in facilitating change, and therefore 'work' can begin on the problem as soon as the client is ready. There is no formal 'socialisation' to the model as in many forms of CBT. Equally there is no formal assessment session besides those measures taken to monitor change, and there is no formal agenda setting. Nevertheless, it is typical for a first session to provide some basic information about the process of therapy (in addition to any administrative matters that are specific to the service). Specifically, we inform clients:

- You can arrange sessions from the slots available whenever is convenient for you, even at short notice. There may be a limit to the length of a session if someone has booked the next slot, but if you need more time, or less time, in future, we can discuss this.
- The sessions will involve asking you to talk about the problems that you want to talk about.
- The therapist will be asking questions during the session to help explore what you want to talk about.
- At times the therapist might ask for feedback from you as to whether the session is going as you would like it to go.
- If you would like any more information then please say. (There is likely to be information available in the form of leaflets or other resources.)

Generally, we find that providing any more information than that above can cause the session to be dominated by logistics or concerns that may not be relevant when the MOL actually begins. We try to focus the session on MOL itself, and any other information on the rationale for the therapy or issues around how the client is experiencing the therapy, we address as they arise. An MOL therapist can ask for feedback on the therapy during a session, especially in the first session. Questions such as:

- 'How is this going for you?'
- 'What is it like talking about your problems like this today?'
- 'How is it going right now?'

help to give the client opportunities to guide the therapist. We have found it useful to ask for explicit feedback at the end of each session too –

- 'Is there anything that you would like different next time?'
- 'Was there anything about this session that wasn't quite right?'

Sometimes, it is the case that the pace of the session was too quick, or too slow, or that the client feels that what they really wanted to talk about was not covered. The therapist can use this type of feedback to alter their style for the remainder of the session, or the following week.

We have also developed some leaflets about MOL and frequently asked questions that can be provided to clients who do have concerns (see Appendix 3). Essentially, this maximises the time in session for MOL itself. A small minority of clients report that they do not want to be asked questions and instead would like to be told what to do or given advice by the therapist. The first tack is to talk about this goal directly and help the clients to discuss why they think that advice from someone else will help them more than generating their own solutions. It can often lead to a fruitful discussion, with the client realising the limits of being told what to do, and its potential for conflict. It is, of course, very plausible to give clients advice about seeking alternative sources of help, particularly in high-risk situations (Mansell 2012) and some of this may be helpful to them and help them regain at least short-term control over their lives. Similarly, it might be that a client realises that to achieve a specific goal, they do not possess a required skill and so they might want to do something to address that issue before continuing therapy along the same track. However, it is important to note that this would no longer be MOL, even though it could be guided by the ideas of control theory. Chapter 6 provides a rationale for these kinds of interventions where loss of control can be a consequence of factors other than goal conflict.

PART 2: PRACTICE

How much treatment and how often to provide it

The issues of how many sessions a client should receive and how often they should receive them is important for many reasons. Clinically, providing too many or too few sessions of psychological treatment is likely to mean an unsatisfactory resolution to the client's psychological distress. Administratively and organisationally, providing sessions inefficiently could contribute to lengthy waiting lists and delays in accessing services. Financially, providing too many sessions is a waste of valuable resources and providing too few sessions could mean that clients are not able to contribute to society and their communities in the ways they would like to.

Despite the importance of these considerations there is little guidance from the literature regarding the ideal treatment protocol. Demonstrations in randomised controlled trials, for example, showing that 12 weekly sessions are an effective time frame (on average) for clients to reduce particular forms of distress are *not* demonstrations that 12 sessions are *necessary or required*. The lack of guidance in the literature, however, does not prevent treatment delivery decisions being made. So how do you decide how often to provide sessions to clients and how do you know when clients have had enough treatment?

The Dose-Response or Dose-Effect model has had a pervasive, albeit sometimes unwitting, influence on the provision of sessions of psychological treatment. The classic paper by Howard *et al.* (1986) suggested that improvement by clients receiving psychological treatment followed a negatively accelerating aggregate curve such that most gains were made in the first few sessions of treatment with more sessions being needed later in treatment to achieve the same degree of improvement. There are nuances to this finding, however, that have been clarified in further research. Barkham and Stiles and their colleagues (e.g. Barkham *et al.* 1996, 2006; Stiles *et al.* 2008) reported that the negatively accelerating curve was a feature of examining aggregated data that is not apparent when individual change trajectories are examined. There are also differences depending on whether endings to the treatment are planned or unplanned. The criterion by which treatment is regarded as finished or successful is also important. Judgements are typically made by therapists and often rely on clients scoring within the normal range on standardised questionnaires of symptomatology.

The Barkham and Stiles group have suggested that a Good Enough Level (GEL) model characterises the data more accurately than the Dose-Effect model. The suggestion here is that clients attend sessions of psychological treatment until they have made the change that they feel is desirable and acceptable. Under the GEL model, the number of sessions that clients attend varies from client to client but the amount of pre-post treatment change remains approximately constant. This model is able to more easily accommodate the non-linear and dynamic nature of the change process. This is no different to the principle of how different people need different time scales in which to learn a new language or to be able to drive a car. In psychotherapy, some clients change quickly and suddenly whereas others change more gradually over a longer period of time. The data from naturalistic studies with unplanned treatment endings appear to support the GEL rather than the Dose-Effect model (Carey 2010).

The GEL model is very compatible with the ethos of MOL in which client control over decision-making is promoted and respected. Based on the PCT understanding of people as living control systems, an MOL clinician considers that clients are not sick or simple. They are 'stuck' in one or more important areas of their lives. It is considered that, for the most part, clients know when something is wrong and they know when they need help. They also know when the 'help' is helping and when it isn't. And they know when they have had enough help and when they want to 'go it alone' again.

Therefore, treatment delivery with MOL is left in the hands of the client unless there is some very compelling evidence for arranging this differently. Practically, this will require being flexible when organising services to establish systems whereby clients can make appointments at their discretion rather than at the suggestion of the clinician. In General Practitioner (GP) practices this can mean having the clinician's timetable on the appointment booking software that the receptionists manage. Clients in this context make appointments to see the clinician in the same way that they make appointments to see their GP. In other settings similar arrangements can be made using web-based resources such as the Calendar in Outlook. For example, if treatment is provided in a hospital outclient setting, the clinician's departmental secretary could have access to the clinician's Outlook Calendar and clients could phone the secretary to make appointments.

This 'client-led' approach to organising treatment sessions has been used extensively with MOL in primary care settings in the NHS (e.g. Carey 2010). The finding that has been replicated with different clinicians, different clients, and across different clinical settings has been that clients generally attend a small average number of sessions. The average might be between four and six sessions with many clients attending a small number of sessions and a few clients accessing many more sessions. There are also a very small number of missed or cancelled appointments (the median is typically zero). With this more flexible approach to treatment delivery, resources have been available to accommodate that small number of clients who seek more sessions than the average.

Using the client-led approach, there has not been a need to cap the number of sessions clients access or to restrict the referrals made by GPs or other health professionals. Dramatic improvements in waiting times, access to services, and service capacity have been observed. The client-led system, however, does raise important professional and ethical issues for clinicians to reconcile. When has a client had enough treatment and who should make that decision? What are our expectations about the sort of lives our clients should be living?

The client-led model offers great promise for services seeking to empower clients and to improve waiting times and access to services. It is not, however, without its challenges. Perhaps the greatest challenge is what it reveals about our own beliefs regarding the capabilities of the clients we seek to help.

PART 2: PRACTICE

24

A focus on distress rather than symptoms

PCT explains that a person controls their experiences as opposed to the actions that help to create the experiences. The focus for MOL, therefore, is on the distress associated with any particular symptom rather than the symptoms themselves. MOL therapists work hard to avoid assuming that they know what their clients will find distressing. At every opportunity they ask clients if what they are describing is what bothers or distresses them.

As we mentioned earlier, it is a curious fact that for any symptom that a person brings along to therapy there are invariably other people with the same kind of experience who do not see it as a problem at all. Some people have time consuming routines but aren't bothered by them. Some people think life is meaningless and pointless but just accept that that's the way it is. Some people hear critical voices but the voices help them focus and be strong. For this reason, when we're using MOL, we like to know about the distress associated with any particular symptom rather than the symptoms themselves. So, if someone came along and told us that they had just lost their job, we might ask 'How does it feel to have just lost your job?' or 'Does it bother you to have just lost your job?' While these might seem like obvious questions, we've found that the answers can be illuminating. The person might say, for example, 'Well it's not the job so much but I don't know how I'm going to look after my brother now'. Or they might say 'Of course it does, I'll never get a job as good as that one'. Or they might say 'You see I quite fancied the girl at the next desk and we were getting along really well and now I'm not going to see her again'. For the example of experiencing critical voices, one person might be bothered because they believe the voice to be a dead relative and this disturbs them; another might not be bothered by what the voice says but is aggravated by its repetitive quality and

101

loud volume, and someone else might find that they cannot focus away from the criticisms and this affects their mood. The point is that for everyone, there will be some unique personal meaning in any problem that occurs. Our job, using MOL, is to help people clarify what that meaning is and the part it plays in the life they want to be living.

A person might express their distress in a variety of ways. They might, for example, talk about a particular image that occurs to them as they are questioned about their distress. Or, they might describe a particular feeling. From a PCT perspective a person's internal experiences can be thought of as perceptions they are creating and, by thinking of these experiences as perceptions, there is not a need to differentiate images, thoughts, feelings and so on. An MOL therapist can move easily between asking about thoughts, images (and other sensory experiences such as sounds, smells and tastes), and feelings.

In response to being asked how they feel about something, or if something bothers them, the client might say that they get a sinking feeling in the pit of their stomach or a heavy feeling on their shoulders that weighs them down. When this occurs the same MOL principles apply – the person would be asked to describe the feeling in more detail and would then be asked about any disruptions that occur as they are describing them. The therapists could begin simply by saying something like 'Tell me some more about this sinking feeling' or even just 'A sinking feeling?' More specific questions might focus on the location of the feeling ('Whereabouts do you feel it?', 'Is it always in the same place?'), dynamic features of the feeling ('What sort of a feeling is it?', 'Does it rise and fall in intensity or is it fairly constant?', 'Does it have a pulsating feeling or some other pattern?'), or the temporal nature of the feeling ('How long does it last?', 'Does it start suddenly at full intensity or does it begin gradually?', 'Is there a particular time of the day that it's more likely to occur?').

The same kinds of specific questions can apply to images as well. They might feel that they are juggling a lot of things at the moment and, as you talk, they might form an image of balls in the air. Questions could include asking about how many balls there are, how close they seem to be, what colours they are, how big they are, how

PART 2: PRACTICE

high they are, how quickly they seem to be moving, how they move (just up and down or in other ways as well), does the number of balls ever change – under what conditions or circumstances, and have they always had these balls that they're juggling. The same kind of questioning can apply to any type of image the person has. The following is another example from the therapy session with 'Lisa' – the client who is distressed over her goal of wanting to be perfect – where her associated image is explored.

Therapist: What came into your mind just then?
Lisa: That I've got tears on my face.
Therapist: Is it that you can feel them? Or you've got some sense of the way you look with tears on your face?
Lisa: Yes, the way that I look.
Therapist: So, what are you seeing as far as that's concerned?
Lisa: Someone who looks imperfect.
Therapist: And is it like looking at a photo?
Lisa: Yes. It's facing me. I can see my face.
Therapist: And how clear is the image?
Lisa: It's getting clearer if I focus on it.
Therapist: And can you bring it a bit closer?
Lisa: Yes.
Therapist: And how close would it be now?
Lisa: Maybe to the side.
Therapist: Oh, so it's not just behind you, it's moved to the side. What; like right beside you?
Lisa: Yes, right here *(client gestures next to her head)*.
Therapist: What do you notice in the image when you kind of look at it now?
Lisa: I just notice that it's clearer.
Therapist: Ok, and what about the face that you see?
Lisa: It still doesn't look perfect.
Therapist: Ok, so how does it look?
Lisa: Tired.
Therapist: And what else?
Lisa: *(Client starts to get tearful.)* It looks anxious.

Therapist:	So a tired, anxious, and not perfect-looking face?
Lisa:	Yes.
Therapist:	And when you hold that image that's just beside you that's a bit clearer and it's looking a bit tired and anxious, what goes through your mind?
Lisa:	Just that I need to calm down and relax a bit more.
Therapist:	Hmm . . . and as we talk about it, you get a bit teary again. . .
Lisa:	Yes, because it's sad. It's sad.
Therapist:	I'm missing the sad bit I think, can you tell me about what it is that's sad?
Lisa:	It's just all the hard work . . . it's weary.
Therapist:	And it's sad to be working that hard?
Lisa:	*(Client is crying.)*
Therapist:	Does it bother you to be sad about it?
Lisa:	Because I think I miss out on things. I miss out on things in life.

As with all MOL questioning, the purpose of asking these kinds of questions about feelings and images is to have the person focus, in detail, on some aspect of their experience so, by doing that, they might become fleetingly aware of higher-level perceptions that could be the clue to the solution to their current problem. Even though the conversation about feelings or images might be rich and interesting, the therapist should be prepared to leave the conversation as soon as they spot a disruption to ask about. An example of this was a lady who was speaking about her plans to move into her new house, but the associated stress was so great that she felt paralysed. She paused mid-sentence, and when asked about this disruption, she said she had experienced a clear image of walking through the front door to the house. As she was questioned further about the image, she started to picture the inside of the new house and described how the rooms looked too small, the paint was peeling off the walls and furniture was falling apart. She suddenly noticed that she felt sad, something she had not previously been aware of as her attention was focused on all the practical behaviours involved in actually moving house. She then exclaimed 'I don't think I even want to live in this house' and decided she needed to consider other alternatives. Following further exploration of this, she described feeling as though a 'weight had been removed from her shoulders'. Some people find it difficult to articulate their feelings and thoughts in words and naturally gravitate to other modalities such as images related to their experiences. We would recommend asking about these other modalities as a way of facilitating a person to be able to focus on a present moment perception.

Of course the 'How do you feel?' or 'Does it bother you?' questioning need not be a one-off event. If you ask the question once and somebody explains that they get a sinking feeling in the pit of their stomach, or a feeling of dread washing over them, or a tightness across their forehead, or a heaviness on their shoulders, or any other feeling, you could ask 'How do you feel about this dread washing over you?' or 'Does it bother you to get this sinking feeling?' Similarly, if someone said that they felt like things were becoming overwhelming and you asked them how they felt about that or if that bothered them, they could reply by explaining with a metaphor that they felt like they were keeping a lot of balls in the air, or standing at the edge of a giant precipice, or being on a rollercoaster that's getting faster and faster. So, you could ask 'How do you feel about being on this rollercoaster?' or 'Does it bother you to be at the edge of this precipice?' Sometimes asking these types of questions more than once in a conversation will help to get to the source of the distress.

People's symptoms often seem to be the main problem. It's certainly not always easy as a therapist to learn about the frightening and debilitating symptoms that your clients experience. PCT suggests, however, that the symptoms are a by-product of the problem rather than the problem itself. The most help we can be to our clients from this point of view is to ask questions and notice disruptions so that their awareness might shift to the higher levels that are generating their difficulties. This can require a certain discipline from the therapist as well as clarity about the maintenance of the client's problem and the way you can be most useful in helping them create effective solutions for themselves.

Outcome monitoring

The issue of what makes an effective clinician effective or, indeed, what can help make a clinician even more effective is an important one and one that is bound to be multi-faceted. It's tempting to think of good clinicians as just 'being born that way' – they seem so natural and effortless at doing what they do. Clinician effectiveness is important to ensure clients are receiving the most efficient treatment possible and, despite the focus on particular treatments that are 'evidence-based', the research indicates that the clinician delivering the treatment tends to have a greater effect on outcomes than the particular treatment being delivered.

There is no doubt, then, that clinician effectiveness is important. What has been much harder to fathom is how to improve effectiveness. An extremely useful paper by Miller *et al.* (2008), however, has shed some light on this area. According to Miller and his colleagues, becoming a highly effective clinician is, in principle, no different from becoming highly expert in any area. An important component in the pursuit of expertness is one's application to the task. Just as elite athletes or concert pianists spend many hours training and practising, so too, highly effective clinicians spend many hours perfecting their craft. They read extensively on the topic, they attend professional development activities and training workshops, they reflect on their practice, and they utilise supervision.

One crucial, but often overlooked, aspect to clinician performance is feedback. Expert clinicians seek feedback from their clients and use this feedback to enhance the therapeutic experience. Because of the importance of regular feedback in terms of clinician effectiveness and enhanced outcomes, in MOL, it is recommended that outcome data are collected at every session.

A number of excellent and easy to use questionnaires exist that have been designed to be used at every session. The Outcome Rating Scale (ORS) and the Session Rating Scale (SRS) (www.talkingcure.com) are a pair of scales that both ask for four ratings to be made. The ORS asks the client to rate how they have experienced the last week in four different areas (individually, interpersonally, socially and overall). The scales are 10cm long and scoring involves simply measuring how far along the line the client has made a mark. Scores range, therefore, from 0 to 40. The SRS is used at the end of the session and asks clients to make four more ratings about their experience of the session in terms of whether or not: they felt heard, understood, respected; if they worked on what they wanted to work on; if the clinician's approach was a good fit for them; and if there was anything missing in the session. There are separate versions for children and youth and a manual that describes the use of the scales.

Perhaps the pioneer and leading world researcher in the area of client feedback is Michael Lambert and, in conjunction with Gary Burlingame, he developed the Outcome Questionnaire (OQ; http://www.oqmeasures.com/). There are a number of different versions of the OQ including a 45-item and a 30-item version, Spanish translations and versions for youth. Again, the OQ is intended to be used at every session and allows clinicians to track the progress of the client.

In the United Kingdom the Clinical Outcome in Routine Evaluation outcome measure (CORE; http://www.coreims.co.uk/) has been developed to quantify client outcomes. The CORE has a range of questionnaires including questionnaires that can be used at every session.

These are only three of the available resources for monitoring client progress. Whichever particular method is used it is important for clinician effectiveness, and to maximise client outcomes, to routinely collect client data. The most effective method seems to be to collect data at every, or nearly every, session.

Sometimes, clinical observations and client self-reports can also be used to complement questionnaire data. Indicators such as changes to the client's grooming or demeanour or even the topics they talk about can give some sense of changes that are being made in their lives. It can be the case with MOL that clients can make changes without really realising it so it is important to collect data and record observations. In one case a man discussed his compulsive trait of moving household items, such as the salt shaker, until things 'felt right'. He estimated doing this about 15 times a day. When he returned for treatment the next week he was asked how many times he had been moving things throughout the week. He looked perplexed and commented that he couldn't recall shifting things at all! As he thought about it some more he recollected that on a couple of days he may have moved things 'about three times'.

On another occasion, after six sessions, a very distressed client said that he was no longer having suicidal thoughts. While this was 'only' the client's self-report, he was also clean shaven for the first time since treatment had commenced. He commented that he had resumed shaving once he decided he wanted to continue living. This combination then, of observation and client self-report, provides strong evidence for important change.

There are good reasons, therefore, to collect data regularly. Change can be unpredictable and sudden and clinician effectiveness seems to be at least partly dependent on regular information from clients.

Evaluating your own practice

Perceptual Control Theory is a way of explaining all kinds of living systems, not simply people with psychological distress. It can certainly be used to try to explain and work with therapists themselves. Therefore, we regard a therapist as possessing a hierarchy of many goals, even though they may only be aware of a very small number of these goals at any one time. Thus, the goal that the therapist is following during therapy at one point (e.g. to listen as hard as possible) exists in the context of other goals within the therapy (e.g. to be curious about what the client is saying, to catch momentary disruptions), and within the context of their own personal goals (e.g. to be a good therapist, to be kind). For this reason, we would expect that MOL questions can be used by another person in conversation with the therapist to supervise or train them. Essentially, we regard the process of developing as a therapist as a process of controlling one's awareness to consider the different levels of goals one possesses, and to adapt them in a way that is adherent to the therapy, and seems fruitful to the clients. This process of change is reorganisation – reprioritising certain goals for therapy, modifying the way that questions are asked and adapting the way one focuses on different disruptions by the clients.

We advocate training in MOL through repeated practice and evaluation by yourself and others. Fortunately, MOL can be used for any 'problem' that a person is willing to discuss – it is not limited to mental health problems. For this reason, extensive practice can be built up through using MOL with colleagues and using rating scales where appropriate. It is not possible to 'role play' MOL as it involves accessing real thoughts and behaviours in the moment as awareness is shifting. Therefore, it is necessary to practice with someone willing to talk about a real situation. We use a range of methods for practice, including:

- Working in pairs where each person takes it in turn to be the 'client' and both parties review the experience periodically: 'How was the session experienced by the client/therapist?'; 'What questions seemed particularly helpful?'; 'What questions seemed less helpful?'; 'What other questions could have been used?'; 'Any other feedback?'
- As above, except a third person observes the session. This helps to provide another source for evaluation and comments. The individuals in the trio rotate.
- One person is a client, and two or more therapists take it in turns to ask MOL questions. In addition to the above models, this helps therapists to witness a range of questions used by others.
- Multiple clients and multiple therapists – or 'round robin'. This model involves several client-therapist pairs, and the therapist moves round to a different client every three to five minutes. This is carried out more to illustrate the fact that the style of questioning in MOL can be more important than the specific therapist and the therapeutic relationship.
- A person on their own can spend time saying out loud the thoughts that are going through their mind. If this activity is sustained for more than a few minutes it will give you a good experience of background thoughts about what you are doing while you are doing it.

Our most common tool in MOL supervision is also MOL itself. We use MOL questions to help therapists talk about the 'problem'. This may be a feature of a recent session that was particularly notable or did not seem to go as expected. We also listen to recordings of sessions and use questioning to help therapists consider the goals behind each question explicitly, and this in turn helps them to generate alternative questions in MOL. We have also developed questionnaires to monitor MOL. These are particularly helpful for establishing competence for practice, for self-evaluation in the absence of supervision, and for research (e.g. Bird *et al.* 2009; Kelly *et al.* 2012). The MOL Adherence Scale and the Self-Evaluation Scale are included in the Appendices. Also, PCT is used in these discussions to attempt to formulate new ideas for questions. For example, there may be a discussion of what the client is trying to control in the session and whether there is conflict that could be identified. In sum, the aims of supervision include:

- To raise awareness of one's own style of questioning during an MOL session.
- To raise awareness of the goals behind one's MOL questions.
- To consider these goals in the light of MOL – are they consistent with the MOL goals? If not, what MOL goal would be more appropriate at this point?
- To raise awareness of alternative ways of achieving MOL goals, which involves attending to wider aspects of the client's experiences and behaviour (disruptions) to generate a broader repertoire of questions.
- To consider any apparent problems or issues raised by the therapist or client.

Ultimately, we regard MOL as a method of questioning that can be applied across individuals, in settings beyond mental health. This may mean that MOL can be used by other helping professions, and also by people in the general public, with and without mental health problems. In this way, training and supervision would become part and parcel of giving and receiving MOL, although to do so, the parties involved would need to be well versed in control theory and the reasoning behind why MOL is perceived to be effective in helping people solve their own problems.

PART 2: PRACTICE

27

The therapeutic relationship: liberated exploration

Throughout this book we have suggested that psychological change is a naturally occurring process that is internal to the client. Essentially, when people allow their attention to be directed and sustained according to their disruptions – often marked by shifts in mood, behaviour, and arousal – they will become more aware of their deeper goals and values. This in turn allows them to apply their normal problem-solving process to these concerns – the specific process termed 'reorganisation' that we have explained. Yet, earlier chapters of this book have also described the kind of environment that the therapist can create, through their stance of curiosity, genuineness, and attentiveness to present moment processes, to facilitate processes of change in the client. It is our view that one of the key components of the 'therapeutic relationship' works in this manner. A good relationship is one that helps the client to talk freely about their problems and allows the client to share their present moment thoughts and feelings and reflect on them (Carey *et al.* 2012). In other words, clients need to be able to speak without trying to filter what they are saying in certain ways which can make it more difficult to free up their awareness to truly focus on what is most significant for them. We propose that this process in itself can be sufficient to promote change and is free from other aspects of the therapeutic relationship that are less clear cut in their impact.

To take one example of a feature of the therapeutic relationship often emphasised, it is thought that the therapist provides a useful model of a relating person that the client can emulate or learn from. Indeed, clients often report that they find qualities of the therapist helpful (e.g. trustworthy, kind) and they look for these qualities in other people outside therapy. But what happens if the therapist (like any person) has their own faults and difficulties in interpersonal style? The client could easily home in on the problematic interpersonal features of the therapist rather than the ones that are helpful. In these instances, guided reflection may be necessary for the client to work out which features of other people are helpful to emulate or attempt to recreate outside the session.

A further, but contrary, view is that the therapist is merely a vehicle for explaining and directing a therapeutic technique and it is only the technique that provides the change we hope for in our clients. Indeed, there are many modalities of therapy such as self-help and computerised therapies that seem to work without a therapist. But, what happens if the technique is not the right match with the client? Does the therapist carry on pushing the technique regardless? This might engender 'resistance' in the client, as they steadfastly refuse to carry out a behavioural experiment or complete homework, for example. These roadblocks are normally bypassed through open discussion of the client's concerns about the intervention, and returning to the overarching (higher-level) goals of the therapy, to find an alternative (lower-level) technique. And so again we come back to the capacity for the therapist to facilitate the client's awareness of their own thoughts, feelings, and goals through talking about them freely thereby facilitating reflection.

Figure 27.1 illustrates a spectrum of interpersonal styles – from excessive control by the therapist to excessive control by the client – with a shared control of experience (convergent goals) in the centre. Note that conflict in goals is never completely absent as we cannot ensure an exact match between two people's reference points for an experience. Yet, it has been demonstrated that people manage to collaborate – to engage in 'collective control' – despite mild conflict (McClelland 2004). Nevertheless, reducing conflict and error, and enhancing overall control is still regarded as the core goal of any living organism.

The central box in the diagram approximates the collaborative exploration that is facilitated by allowing clients to talk freely about their problems and reflect on present experiences through the curious and open stance of the therapist. This is standard practice in MOL.

PART 2: PRACTICE

How does therapy facilitate change?

Therapist goals ⟷ Convergence in goals ⟷ Client goals

| **Arbitrary control by therapist** (attempts that circumvent the problem or cause conflict with client) | **Therapist directs change** (techniques to focus on problem, develop new skills) | **Therapist shows empathic curiosity** (minimal arbitrary control, curious, shared exploration of problem, focused on present) | **Client directs change** (client talks about problem, focuses on present, or discusses coping) | **Arbitrary control by client** (leads to conflict with, or compliance from, the therapist) |

Enabling flexible control? (shift of attention to conflict and sustained awareness to facilitate effective reorganisation)

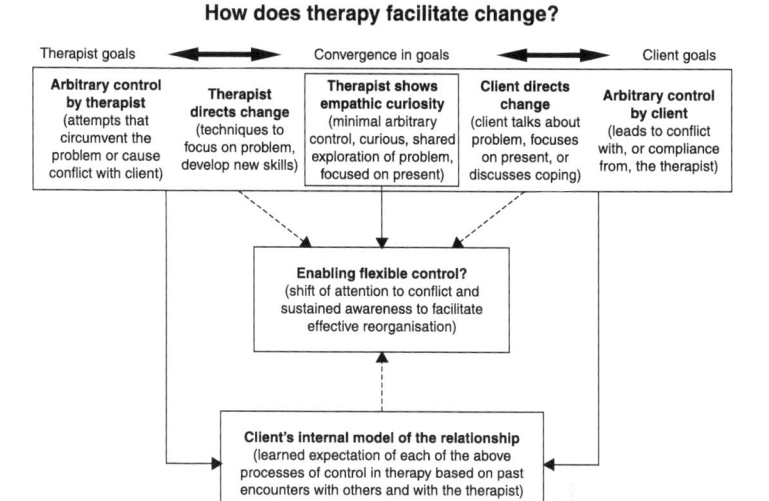

Client's internal model of the relationship (learned expectation of each of the above processes of control in therapy based on past encounters with others and with the therapist)

Figure 27.1 A model of how balancing goals in the therapeutic relationship facilitates change.

The arrow from this box to 'enabling flexible control' illustrates that this stance is regarded as most efficient and least problematic in facilitating change. It is also acknowledged in this diagram that directive attempts at employing techniques such as exposure or behavioural activation, can sometimes promote effective change, as can learned models of the therapeutic relationship. However, they are dotted in the diagram to indicate that they may have more limitations in causing further conflict if they are not carefully applied to the client's current goals. Therefore, these facets of the relationship are often supplemented by periods of returning to open enquiry, collaborative discussion and attentiveness to the client's thoughts and feelings that emerge in the present moment.

The rationale we have provided here confirms why the process of MOL is designed the way it has been described in this book. It also provides an opportunity to see the relevance of MOL within other therapies and interventions. It can be used within other interventions to help ensure that they are guided according to the client's wishes and yet in a way that can be seen as constructive in fulfilling higher-level goals, rather than temporary, inflexible attempts at regaining control that may be counterproductive.

This model can also be used in supervision of MOL to explore where therapy is deviating from the gold standard of MOL. When difficulties do arise within therapy, it is often the case that there is conflict between the therapist's goals and those of the client. As a therapist, it is possible to lose awareness of when you might be making interpretations and assumptions about the clients' experiences and what might be helpful for them from your own perspective. Most of us can relate to moments with a client where we have thought 'if only they (the client) could see it from this point of view'; 'if only they would use this particular solution'; 'if only . . . '. However, the essence of MOL is in facilitating the shift of the client's awareness to his or her own solutions. Supervision is a good place to help a therapist reflect on their own goals and be more aware of when they might conflict with those of the client and thus unintentionally 'get in the way' of the therapeutic process.

Our most common question when supervising MOL is exactly that – 'What was your goal as a therapist?' Essentially, we are expecting that the answer will be one of the two goals of MOL – to help the client talk about their problem or to notice disruptions and bring them to the client's attention. Yet, we often find that the therapist's goal has drifted – 'To get them to realise that what they are doing is making their problem worse'; 'To get them better quicker'; 'To get them to calm down'; 'To get them to understand their problems'; and 'To not look rude and intrusive' are some examples. Each of these goals may lead the client to be controlled in a specific way by the therapist – a way that is not merely to facilitate their awareness. For example, the client whose therapist wants them to get better quicker may experience MOL questions as too intrusive. The client whose therapist wants them to understand their problems may find that their answers become more intellectual and less attached to their current feelings. The clients themselves may or may not be aware of this arbitrary control that is gearing the direction of the conversation and their internal experiences. Supervision for MOL involves helping therapists to notice these implicit (and sometimes explicit) goals in their own questioning. After doing so, the aim is to reiterate the original goals of MOL, and to work with the supervisor (or peer team) to generate a range of alternative ways to pursue them. For example, a therapist who tends to try to get clients better as quickly as possible may need to learn to pace their questions or work on questions that explore present moment experiences in more detail. Therapists who have the goal of not looking rude and intrusive can experiment with asking questions more regularly, or may be openly asking the client if it is OK to ask more questions.

As therapists, we are normal people who have our own array of goals that we use in our everyday lives. These can be brought into therapy sessions. Occasionally they align well with the goals of MOL (e.g. if a therapist's goal in everyday life is to listen to what people have to say). Yet, most of the time our everyday goals do not align with those of being a therapist and create conflict with the goals of MOL. They potentially also create conflict with client's goals, just like the client's own attempts at arbitrary control. Of course, it is also likely to be the case that a therapist's goals will sometimes converge very neatly with certain client groups. This might explain why we see therapists specialising in such narrow domains. But as MOL is a transdiagnostic therapy for all, this bias would restrict its applicability. Therapists, just like clients, need an environment to discuss the therapy session openly and attend to any problems. PCT would model therapists in exactly the same way as clients. Through appropriate questioning, reorganisation is thought to work in therapists' own control hierarchies and enable them to engage in more flexible control to work with their clients more effectively.

PART 2: PRACTICE

Building MOL into other therapies and therapeutic practices

MOL is designed as a stand-alone therapy because it addresses a process of change – shifting awareness to the higher-level goals driving conflict – that is proposed to underlie chronic psychological distress. In Chapter 6, we explained that the loss of control driving distress can have other causes that are not addressed by MOL, such as stressors in the client's environment that are outside the client's capacities for control. Therefore, under some circumstances, it may be possible to blend MOL with other interventions. A second reason for blending MOL is that clinicians, comfortable and skilled in their existing modalities, may feel unsure about switching approaches. The succinct and simple nature of MOL means that it is particularly easy to interweave with other therapies. In fact, many new MOL therapists begin with just the occasional MOL question during their usual CBT practice.

For those of you who would like to use MOL more sparingly in this way for now, we can provide some indication of when it might be particularly helpful to use MOL. We will cover several instances. The first range of situations exploits the capacity for MOL to draw out self-directed goals that may conflict with one another and include agenda setting, ambivalence, 'resistance', and preparation for change. The second range of situations draws upon the capacity for MOL questions to focus on the client's present moment perception and includes idiosyncratic experiences, emotional processing, and getting 'stuck' in therapy.

Ideally, the role of the agenda in CBT is to ensure that the client and therapist agree on goals for the session that are important to the client and within the remit of the therapy, and the expertise of the therapist, to discuss and address. This means that the content for the agenda should typically be driven by the client, even though the process itself is facilitated by the therapist. However, there are many instances where this ideal may be a challenge: the client cannot decide on what to talk about or suggests that the therapist should set the agenda; there are too many items; or the items are difficult to prioritise. It is tempting in these instances for the therapist to take the reins and decide for the client what will be on the agenda. MOL provides an alternative, because it is guided by the principle that everyone can make their own choices, once their awareness is directed to the relevant thoughts and feelings. Here are some examples:

Client: There are so many things to discuss, I don't know where to start.

Example Therapist questions:

- 'How does it feel not knowing where to start?'
- 'Which things are in your mind right now as you are thinking about it?'
- 'Are some things clearer than other things right now?'
- 'How many things are in your head right now?'

Each of these questions gently puts the ownership of deciding the agenda back to the client, but in a way that helps the client think about it further, and in a more complete manner. It is a learned skill to allow one's mind to enter a mode that aids decision-making, and one that the client may benefit from outside the session. In our experience, MOL questions always gravitate to one topic that really does reflect a relevant concern of the client, even if it might not be the topic that both parties had initially anticipated.

MOL deals with several elements of therapy that seem to share the assumption that the client should be moving in a certain direction. Ambivalence about therapy is driven by the assumption that the client should be coming to therapy. 'Resistance' is driven by the assumption that the client should be engaged in the interventions that the therapist suggests. On a related point, it is commonly recognised that change techniques in CBT are not always acceptable to clients and that they require preparation, including a rationale, formulation, and planning. MOL and PCT do not make the same assumptions. It is understood that the client can be in conflict over whether to attend or miss a therapy appointment, whether to continue or drop a damaging habit or safety behaviour, or whether to face or avoid an intervention such as exposure or behavioural experiments. MOL questions can encourage open discussions about the two sides of the decision; whether or not one side is regarded as more desirable or therapeutic. Here are some examples:

Client: If we have this role play planned for next week, I will have to really push myself hard.
Therapist: What makes you say you will need to push yourself?
What do you think you would be pushing against?
How hard do you really want to push yourself at the moment?
When you think of the role play next week, what are you imagining?
How does it feel talking about the plan for next week?

(These numerous examples are provided to demonstrate the range of questions that are possible. The therapist would not ask all these questions at the same time.)

These questions are designed to help the client reveal their ambivalence about the intervention, and to look deeper into their concerns, illustrating that they are valid. MOL itself does not include elaborate techniques nor assume that the therapist's expectations of when attendance, and psychological change, should occur are valid. Nevertheless, it can at least set the stage so that only those clients who genuinely understand the intervention and their own concerns about it will engage in the intervention in an open and transparent manner. Indeed, it would not seem ethical to coerce or force an intervention on a client in the absence of a discussion of this kind.

PCT proposes that our behaviour controls our perception, and because perception is a private phenomenon, we can only strive to try to understand what another person is experiencing. Assumptions based on what we have been told, what we have read, or on our own experiences, may well be inaccurate. This stance frees up the MOL therapist to ask enquiringly about what is going on for the client, without searching for a fixed idea of what they expect to hear. For example, an MOL therapist would not expect that any thought described by a client who had experienced psychosis would be 'delusional' and they would not expect a client with an anxiety disorder to be only bothered about anxiety – other moods such as anger and grief might be more important right now. MOL questions help clients describe experiences in their own words, often using imagery and metaphors. Therefore, MOL questions can be used within other therapeutic approaches whenever a therapist gets 'stuck' in their line of questioning and when the client's experiences don't seem to match the planned 'model'.

MOL questions that home in on present moment experiences also have the capacity to transform a conversation that is becoming overly intellectual and abstract to one that is grounded in the client's lived experience. This is one example of where MOL can deviate from typical Socratic questioning. For example, suppose a client rolls her eyes and says 'I worry all the time!' Some MOL questions to this statement can be relatively abstract such as 'What do you mean by worry?', 'How much is all the time?' However, more experiential MOL questions would include 'How much are you worrying right now?', 'How does it feel to say that out loud?' and 'What makes you roll your eyes when you say that?' These questions provide opportunities to engage emotions, bringing what is known to be an overly abstract process – worry – into the lived present. It may also help a client to express how they really feel about their worry rather than the overly rehearsed answers and truisms they might typically tell themselves, such as 'worrying is bad' and 'it is best not to worry'. Deeper feelings around worry might involve fears of going mad, as a reason for worrying less, and in conflict with this, goals for worrying more, such as 'it is my only way to cope' and 'it stops me thinking about the trauma I experienced'. Once these higher-level goals are accessed, the client may feel able to talk more freely about their concerns in a way that rarely arises from an intellectual discussion about worry.

PART 2: PRACTICE

In all therapy, including MOL, therapists can get 'stuck'. They may not know what question to ask next. They may feel that all avenues have been covered and that there are no more problems they have expertise to address. Yet, according to PCT, if the client is returning for therapy, returning for therapy must serve a goal that they hold. There are a whole range of MOL questions that can be used when things appear stuck. They each refocus the client's attention on their concerns and their experiences right now. Here are some examples:

- 'How has it been going talking about things today?'
- 'What's going on for you right now?'
- 'Is there anything important that we haven't mentioned yet today?'

According to PCT, our attention will naturally drift to where there is 'error' – in other words where there is a problem – if we are helped to talk freely, and catch our thoughts and feelings as they emerge. Therefore, these kinds of questions, although simple, keep that opportunity for the most relevant problems to be discussed, rather than curtailing the conversation or resorting to topics, selected by the therapist, that may not be most relevant to the client.

This chapter has been guided by a sense of realism – that most therapists do not abandon their existing repertoire for the chance that a novel theory and therapy will be more effective. Most clinicians in everyday practice report being 'eclectic' to some degree, drawing on what they perceive to be the most useful elements of several approaches. We cannot make a judgment about whether such eclecticism is necessary, or more effective. However, we are fortunate that MOL does lend itself well to being built into other therapies. This may provide a starting point for a fuller adoption of MOL as a therapy and PCT as a guiding set of principles.

Utilising control theory in existing CBT

A control theory approach is in no way specific to explaining and justifying MOL as a sole intervention. The theory can be used to understand, and potentially enhance, existing interventions in CBT, and other therapies. This would particularly be the case for elements of CBT that would seem to benefit from a theoretical explanation beyond those that are normally provided. In this section we summarise several components of existing CBT that we have touched upon in previous chapters to show how PCT can attempt to integrate these components under a single framework. They are: agenda setting, the collaborative relationship, decentring, exposure, activity scheduling, and behavioural experiments.

We discussed how to use MOL in agenda setting in the last chapter. In this chapter we delve further into the theory behind why and how an agenda might work according to PCT. Setting an agenda occurs at the start of every CBT session. But why might an agenda be so important, and can the procedure be enhanced? From a control theory perspective, the agenda helps the client to articulate and prioritise their *goals* for the session. Because all behaviour is goal-directed, opportunities to express one's goals make the session meaningful for the client. Yet, we have seen how goals are organised at multiple levels according to the theory, with the higher-level goals (e.g. to be a worthwhile person) having influence over how lower-level goals (e.g. to do more activities) are set. This implies that agendas for therapy may be more fruitful when they help address these higher-order goals. For example, the first item on the agenda may be to 'try to do day–to-day tasks around the house'. The therapist can ask 'What makes this important to you?' to help identify the higher-level goal. The client might answer 'to be a good husband', for example. One advantage of discussing higher-level goals is that

127

it frees up choices for different (lower-level) *means* of achieving the goal. In this example, the therapist and client could discuss other ways to be a 'good husband' in addition to doing day-to-day tasks (e.g. 'to listen to my wife's worries'); or it may help to identify which tasks are more important in achieving this goal. It is of course critical to PCT that there are likely to be even deeper goals that make 'being a good husband' important, and this 'upward exploration' provides further opportunities for the client's choices. Similarly, there are times when clinicians are concerned that a client's goal on the agenda might not be achievable. For example, one of our clinicians once reported in supervision that she felt unsure how it would be possible to work with her client's goal – which was to not have a diagnostic label of schizophrenia – as her client had already had the diagnostic label for 20 years! However, through exploring *why* this was a problem, awareness of the associated higher-level goals became apparent. Understandably, the client did not want the label because she anticipated that other people would make negative assumptions about her; and she didn't want such assumptions because she wanted people to think positively about her; and she needed this because she wanted to form good relationships with others. Now there was a tangible goal they could work on?

A control theory perspective can also aid our understanding of what makes a therapeutic relationship effective (Carey *et al.* 2012; Mansell 2012). It is an interesting aspect of CBT that the collaborative nature of the relationship is given pivotal importance. But why? If we return to one of the principles of PCT, that people need to be in control of what matters to them, then it follows that the client needs to feel in control of the important elements of a therapy session. Yet, at the same time, the therapist needs to be in control too – to know what questions to ask and to maintain a sense of structure to the session. If two people are controlling completely *different* experiences from one another, then there is little room for conflict, but also very little connection or influence going either way. In contrast, if two people try to control the *same* experience as one another, but have very different standards for this experience (e.g. the therapist wants the client to feel a high level of anxiety to 'process emotions', but the client wants to feel no anxiety at all), then conflict ensues. This may appear as 'resistance' to the therapist. Control theory tells us that people work well together when they have very similar internal standards – this is known as *collective control* (McClelland 2004). A PCT approach would propose, therefore, that a good collaborative relationship is one allowing an open discussion about which goals can be shared (e.g. to talk about feelings of anxiety), and which cannot be shared right now (e.g. to provoke high levels of anxiety during exposure). This may appear as 'collaboration' and it can be fully modelled using PCT. To take one example of using a familiar technique, it is very probable that the two-way discussion that ensues when planning a graded hierarchy of exposure represents the product of this discussion about which goals can be managed sooner and agreed upon, and which might be faced later. Carey *et al.* (2012) further describe the clinical implications of taking a control theory view of the therapeutic relationship in more detail.

The mindset that MOL attempts to help a client cultivate is one in which they feel sufficiently in control to articulate their current experiences to the therapist, and yet to be increasingly aware of fleeting thoughts and feelings that the therapist identifies as disruptions. In MOL, it is also beneficial if the client can attend to any conflicting goals they have, and sustain their attention on these long enough to allow reorganisation to generate satisfactory solutions. Although this is a spontaneous process, it is experienced by the client as noticing insights, reappraisals, changes in mental imagery, and shifts in perspective. We believe that the mindset being described here is closely related to the states variously described as 'decentring', 'mindfulness', and 'metacognitive awareness'. Thus, where some other forms of CBT use training procedures to cultivate these states, Method of Levels uses ongoing questioning, rather like 'thought catching' in early cognitive therapy (Beck 1967). Yet in PCT, the process of change – reorganisation of goal conflict – is regarded as the *same process* across these wide domains.

Following on from the above account, Carey (2011b) has proposed that exposure therapy involves the same process as described here, and that interventions such as person-centred counselling and emotion-focused therapy actually utilise the same change mechanisms as behavioural and cognitive therapies. They each shift and maintain awareness on to thoughts and feelings that are related to conflicting goals. A control theory view considers that the anxious client, for example, is experiencing conflict between perhaps wanting to approach their fears in order to overcome them, and wanting to avoid their fears to stay feeling safe. Therefore, during any kind of exposure therapy, this 'dance' between approach and avoidance can be discussed with the client. Rather than the therapist taking the role of the 'approach' side of the conflict, the therapist can help to draw out the two sides within the client, and therefore maintain a strong sense of collaboration rather than coercion.

A further common component of CBT, especially in depression, is activity scheduling. In PCT, 'activities' would map onto the lower-level goals in a hierarchy – the programs and sequences of processes that implement our higher-order goals. Activities are integral in implementing and defining higher-level goals. For example, we may gain a sense of being a helpful person through perceiving our own ongoing activities such as doing housework, giving to charity, listening to people, etc. Thus, according to PCT, effective activity scheduling works because it fulfils people's deeper goals and informs their self-concept. It also provides a sense of purpose and control. Taking this into account, activity scheduling can be easily tied into the targets for *cognitive* approaches – helping people to form and maintain more positive views of the self and world. Thus, activity schedules can be built around a formulation that validates people's goals. 'How?' questions help clients to generate activities that may support their goals, and 'Why?' questions help clients to identify the personally relevant reasons for engaging in activities.

We can also apply the above model to behavioural experiments (Mansell 2012). It is commonly accepted that a successful behavioural experiment couples the experiment itself with planning and discussion of the broader reasons and implications of the experiment (Bennett-Levy *et al*. 2004). For example, after making a plan with the therapist, a client with social fears may talk to a stranger for the first time and find out that the new acquaintance does not criticise them as predicted. The therapist asks the client a 'downward arrow question': 'What might this mean about you as a person?' A fruitful insight from the client would be 'It could mean I am more likeable than I had thought'. Thus, again we see that actions in the moment are tied to higher-level goals, and that discussions around these goals help the client to 'generalise' to wider situations (Mansell 2011). It is worth noting a semantic point here – 'downward arrow questions' in CBT and 'exploring higher levels' in MOL are actually in the *same* direction as one another because they both tend towards *deeper* goals and constructs.

It is important to note one key feature of PCT that helps to explain why specific techniques may not always work. One of the most common stumbling blocks in either activity scheduling or behavioural experiments will be conflict. For example, a client with fears of leaving the house may agree to start to take longer walks outside, but at the same time fears the consequences of doing so and wants to return home. So the client might not be 'deliberately' obstructing the therapeutic process – they might just be in conflict. Thus, as we discussed above, MOL questions can be used to explore this conflict when it emerges, helping the client to see both sides in their mind's eye, and drawing the therapist out of any attempts at coercion within the session. This aspect of MOL actually gels with therapies that are often used to enhance CBT for people experiencing conflict over therapy, such as Motivational Interviewing.

A group form of MOL is now being trialled which, like individual MOL, uses PCT to target the key mechanisms of distress and change that were described previously. Group facilitators, through a variety of exercises, help clients to bring their awareness to the source of their problem so that reorganisation can occur and control can be restored – just like in MOL. Facilitators also help clients to access their higher-level goals and values. The group, called the 'Take

Control Group', incorporates the 'client led' approach described in previous chapters. Clients are able to choose how many sessions they attend and whether they attend sessions on consecutive weeks; facilitators provide information on the themes of each session in advance and allow clients to decide whether the session seems relevant to them.

Those of you who have been reading closely will realise that there could be a risk during a group session that clients will perceive that the facilitator is controlling the session ('arbitrary control') – because the group facilitator will have to respond to a range of goals from different clients. However, there are a number of steps taken to minimise the potential for arbitrary control by facilitators including: the emphasis throughout the group on giving clients the opportunity to apply concepts and exercises to themselves, and the facilitator taking regular feedback from clients which shapes subsequent material covered. This is also offset by potential benefits conferred by the group format. For example, groups provide an environment where participants can gain environmental feedback that their goals and experiences are normal and shared with other people. We will see in the future how the Take Control Groups are evaluated and developed in practice.

In sum, we propose that PCT can be used to substantiate and adapt existing techniques in CBT, and potentially other psychotherapies. This avenue is promising from both a scientific and a practical perspective. MOL itself is designed to be a universal therapy, flexibly adapted to the individual's concerns. Yet, there might be times when a specific technique from CBT matches a client's goals particularly well, and could be interweaved with MOL, whilst still being true to a control theory model of the therapeutic process as a whole. This propensity for control theory to explain the mechanisms of change in existing therapies also allows therapists encountering PCT for the first time to 'try it on for size'. They may use control theory ideas to adapt what they do right now, and save the training in MOL as a future opportunity.

Interventions without talking: testing the controlled variable

MOL involves talking, yet control theory is not a theory of speech. It can be used to model speech generation (e.g. Moore 2007), and speech may be essential to certain 'modes' of control (such as planning in the imagination mode; Powers 1973; 2005). Yet, the fundamentals of control do not rely on the spoken word. Indeed the core principles of the theory are seen to apply across species, and therefore outside the realm of spoken or written language. They even extend to biological processes such as homeostasis.

It is worth remembering that control is not dependent on language when doing any kind of spoken therapy. Words may be a form of control and they may tell us about control, but are *not necessarily an accurate picture of what is being controlled*. The client can only report what they are aware of controlling at the moment and not the myriad of internal standards they have for other aspects of their life. The client may have reasons (other goals) for using particular words or describing their experiences in a certain way to the therapist (e.g. emphasising their worries in order to receive reassurance from the therapist). This is one reason why asking about disruptions, such as tone of voice, can be so fruitful in MOL. At its most obvious, a client may be lying to the therapist, or to themselves, and therefore simply not telling their experience as it is. They may have good reasons to do this – such as denying a problem exists because they are not ready to talk about it right now. Interestingly, clients receiving MOL often report that it feels 'honest' and they like this aspect of the therapy. MOL seems to facilitate openness and honesty. However, complete openness and a transparent view of one's own goals is in no way guaranteed.

We covered earlier how to use MOL to work with people who find it hard to put their experiences into words – how to ask questions about 'not knowing what to talk about', for example. Yet, there are groups of clients for whom we might not expect this to generate useful avenues of intervention. These include young children, people with learning disabilities that impact on the use of language, and people who remain unwilling to speak, such as cases of 'elective mutism'. What tools does PCT provide here?

The mark of control in a human or a fellow animal is that a perceptual experience is being kept within a desired range despite environmental disturbances. Normally, our actions are used to act on the environment to achieve this. This has led to the development of a technique to test what an individual is controlling, called the *Test for the Controlled Variable* (TCV) (Powers 1973; 2005; Marken 1980; 2009). Essentially, if we disturb a perception that is controlled by an individual, then we would expect to see an action being used to restore that perception to its reference state. If the variable is not being controlled, we would expect the individual to acquiesce to our attempts and not use their actions to try to restore it. Thus, as health professionals, we can develop a hypothesis around what a client could be controlling and carry out monitoring of the circumstances involved in control; we develop a 'mini-experiment' to test it using the TCV. This application of PCT to interventions is in its infancy, but some examples can be used to illustrate it.

Take the example of a young child who has been identified as being disruptive in class, running around the room and, at worst, hitting other children. The PCT practitioner's first plan of action would be to talk to the child, but the child refuses to speak to her. Therefore, for now, she asks the teacher to use a table to monitor the circumstances surrounding each 'disruption of class' – what is the teacher doing?; what are the other children doing?; what behaviours preceded the event? The practitioner analyses these data. In each case the disruptive behaviour occurs when the children are told by the teacher to work alone in silence. This generates hypotheses around a number of controlled variables: level of noise (set at a level of noise above silence for the pupil); level of social interaction (set at a level of interaction with other children that is not alone); level of work (set at a level lower than that desired by the teacher); and level

PART 2: PRACTICE

of instruction (set at a level below being instructed in the style the teacher uses). These hypotheses are elaborated in Table 30.1.

It is interesting and important to note that some behaviours may fulfil more than one goal (e.g. shouting is self-generated, breaks the

Table 30.1 An example of how Testing the Controlled Variable can be utilised in practice.

Hypothesised Controlled Variable	Explanation	Further Questions	Test
Loudness	The child wants more loudness than the teacher or the other children want.	Does the child disrupt other children when there is lots of ambient noise in the room?	A prolonged period of silence would lead to attempts to break the silence (e.g. shouting).
Social Interaction	The child wants more time interacting with others.	Does the child disrupt other children when they are in a group task?	A prolonged period alone would lead to attempts to seek social interaction (e.g. looking for other children).
Work	The child wants to do a smaller amount of work than the other children.	Does the child disrupt other children when asked to keep silent but not asked to work?	A prolonged period of work would lead to attempts to reduce time spent on the work (e.g. saying it is finished when it is not).
Instruction	The child does not want to follow instructions.	Does the child disrupt other children when engaged in his or her own chosen activities?	Giving instructions would lead to more self-generated activities.

silence and distracts from working). It is also the case that more than one variable is being controlled. Nevertheless, the TCV can provide ideas for intervention. For example, if the child is only controlling the level of social interaction, then further opportunities could be provided for working in groups. This finding then also serves to ask further questions that draw from PCT too. Why does this child require so much social interaction at school? What higher-order goals might the greater social interaction serve? How are these goals being fulfilled more generally in the child's life? These questions can provide further directions for systemic interventions. Again, we have not developed family and systemic interventions for mental health problems using PCT although some tentative possibilities are suggested in Carey and Carey (2001). Yet, the application of PCT to sociology (e.g. McClelland 2004) and organisations (e.g. Vancouver 2000) are promising in setting the foundations.

In summary, we have endeavoured to explain Perceptual Control Theory in an accessible way that is sufficiently detailed to justify and explain the interventions that follow from the theory. We have introduced Method of Levels as the tried and tested manner in which to use PCT to facilitate change using one-to-one therapy across a range of presenting problems and client groups. We have also suggested ways of using PCT and MOL in existing therapies. Finally, we have opened a window to using PCT for wider interventions, including non-verbal analyses of behaviour as controlled perception, and how control can play out in group, or systemic, contexts. If you start to find our rationale persuasive and our methods effective, then we encourage you to continue further informing yourself about PCT and MOL with the many publications and demonstrations available. The ultimate aim of PCT is a scientific movement to establish a new paradigm – a more accurate, empirical science of mental life (Marken 2009). This may take decades, or even centuries, to be achieved, and it will only do so with the collaboration of teams of researchers and self-evaluating practitioners. New evidence may result in changes to the original theory. Yet the direction is clear: living things are purposeful – and yet understandable – and that includes each and every one of us.

Appendix 1

APPENDIX 1

MOL Session Evaluation – Self

T. A. Carey and S. J. Tai

1. To what extent was the content of the session generated by the patient?
   1   2   3   4   5   6   7   8   9   10
   not at all   completely

2. To what extent did the therapist question rather than advise, suggest, or teach?
   1   2   3   4   5   6   7   8   9   10
   not at all   totally

3. To what extent did the therapist ask about disruptions?
   1   2   3   4   5   6   7   8   9   10
   not at all   constantly

4. To what extent did the therapist ask detailed and specific questions about the current topic of conversation?
   1   2   3   4   5   6   7   8   9   10
   not at all   constantly

5. To what extent did the therapist question rather than assume?
   1   2   3   4   5   6   7   8   9   10
   not at all   extremely

6. To what extent did the therapist ask about the patient's immediate experience?
   1   2   3   4   5   6   7   8   9   10
   not at all   constantly

7. To what extent did the therapist follow rather than lead the client?
   1   2   3   4   5   6   7   8   9   10
   not at all   constantly

8. To what extent did the therapist facilitate the client sustaining a focus in one or more areas?
   1   2   3   4   5   6   7   8   9   10
   not at all   constantly

9. Comments about the session:

10: Suggestions for improvement and development:

MOL Session Evaluation – Other

T. A. Carey and S. J. Tai

1. To what extent was the content of the session generated by the patient?
    1   2   3   4   5   6   7   8   9   10
    not at all   completely
    Examples:

2. To what extent did the therapist question rather than advise, suggest, or teach?
    1   2   3   4   5   6   7   8   9   10
    not at all   totally
    Examples:

3. To what extent did the therapist ask about disruptions?
    1   2   3   4   5   6   7   8   9   10
    not at all   constantly
    Examples:

4. To what extent did the therapist ask detailed and specific questions about the current topic of conversation?
    1   2   3   4   5   6   7   8   9   10
    not at all   constantly
    Examples:

5. To what extent did the therapist question rather than assume?
    1   2   3   4   5   6   7   8   9   10
    not at all   extremely
    Examples:

6. To what extent did the therapist ask about the patient's immediate experience?
    1   2   3   4   5   6   7   8   9   10
    not at all   constantly
    Examples:

7. To what extent did the therapist follow rather than lead the client?
    1   2   3   4   5   6   7   8   9   10
    not at all   extremely

8. To what extent did the therapist facilitate the client sustaining a focus in one or more areas?
    1   2   3   4   5   6   7   8   9   10
    not at all   constantly

9. Comments about the session:

10. Suggestions for improvement and development:

APPENDIX 1

MOL Session Evaluation – Behavioural Indicators

T. A. Carey and S. J. Tai

1. Therapist asks something like 'What would you like to talk about today?' Therapist discusses topics that the patient nominates.

2. Absence of advice or suggestions. When asked by the patient for advice the therapist continues to use MOL by asking things like: 'Are you wondering what you should be doing just now?', 'What made that question pop into your head at this moment?', 'What sort of advice do you think would be helpful for you just now?'. A ratio in the range of perhaps 6:1 to 8:1 for the number of questions to statements.

3. The therapist picks up on disruptions in the patient's flow of speech and asks things like: 'What's going through your mind just now?', 'What were you thinking when you paused just then?', 'What were you shaking your head about while you were talking just now?'.

4. The questions the therapist asks sound curious rather than rhetorical. Process as well as content questions are asked; there is a preponderance of questions that invite concrete rather than abstract answers like: 'How many times does X occur?', 'When you're feeling X, what else do you notice?', 'Does Y ever happen when you're thinking Z?', 'How big is it?', 'What colour is it?', 'Does it have a shape?', 'Are there edges to it?', 'How do you know when W is starting to happen?', 'When you feeling Y, does it come on suddenly or gradually?', 'Is it a constant feeling or does it fluctuate or pulsate or change in some other way?'.

5. The therapist asks questions that might appear obvious or simplistic, the therapist routinely clarifies the meanings of words and checks for understanding. Questions like the following would be asked: 'When you say "depression" what do you mean by that?', 'You called your thoughts bad just now, what's the bad aspect to the thoughts you're referring to?', 'When you say X are you meaning something like Y?', 'Does Z go along with W?'.

6. The therapist draws the patient's attention to the thoughts and feelings that occur for the patient as they discuss the patient's nominated topics. Questions such as the following would be expected: 'What's going through your mind as you describe these events to me?', 'What occurs to you when you express things that way?', 'What do you think when you hear yourself say that?', 'Are you comparing X and Y just now?', 'Is there something you're avoiding or trying not to think about while we're talking?'.

7. The therapist explores the topics and issues that the client provides. The therapist also discusses the topics in a way that seems to be indicated by the client and acknowledges and accommodates aspects such as the pace of the client's dialogue. If the client talks about images, the therapist asks questions about images, if the client talks about feelings the therapist asks about feelings, and so on.

8. Through systematic questioning, the therapist helps the client maintain their focus on a particular topic for a sustained period of time. For example, even with a disruption the therapist might ask 3 or 4 questions about the disruption rather than just one.

Appendix 2

APPENDIX 2

Method of Levels Adherence Scale (MOLAS: Version 3)

W. Mansell, T. A. Carey, T. Bird, S. J. Tai, R. J. Mullan and C. G. Spratt

Name: _____   Scorer: _____

Date: _____   Session: _____

MOL ADHERENCE SCALE – MOLAS

The rating of the scale

The present seven point scale (i.e. a 0–6 Likert scale) extends from (0) where the therapist did not adhere to that aspect of therapy (non-adherence) to (6) where there is adherence and very high skill. Thus the scale assesses both adherence to therapy method and skill of the therapist. To aid with the rating of items on the scale, an outline of the key features of each item is provided at the top of each section. A description of the various rating criteria is given in the right hand margin – see example overleaf in Figure 1. Further details are provided in the accompanying manual.

The examples are intended to be used as useful guidelines only. They are not meant to be used as prescriptive scoring criteria, rather providing both illustrative anchor points and guides.

The '**Key Features**' describe the important features that need to be considered when scoring each item. When rating the item, you must first identify whether some of the features are present. You must then consider whether the therapist should be regarded as competent with the features. If the therapist includes most of the key features and uses them appropriately (i.e. misses few relevant opportunities to use them), the therapist should be rated very highly.

APPENDIX 2

Figure 1: Example of the scoring layout

Key features: this is an operationalised description of the item (see examples within the scale).

Mark with an 'X' on the vertical line, using whole and half numbers, the level to which you think the therapist has fulfilled the core function. The descriptive features on the right are designed to guide your decision.

	Competence level	Examples
Incompetent	0	absence of feature, or highly inappropriate performance
Novice	1	inappropriate performance, with major problems evident
Advanced beginner	2	evidence of competence, but numerous problems and lack of consistency
Competent	3	competent, but some problems and/or inconsistencies
Proficient	4	good features, but minor problems and/or inconsistencies
Expert	5	very good features, minimal problems and/or inconsistencies
	6	excellent performance, or very good even in the face of patient difficulties

* The present scale has incorporated the Dreyfus system (Dreyfus, 1989) for denoting competence. Please note that the top marks (i.e. near the 'expert' end of the continuum) are reserved for those therapists demonstrating highly effective skills, particularly in the face of difficulties (i.e. highly aggressive or avoidant patients; high levels of emotional discharge from the patients; and various situational factors).

The '**Examples**' are only guidelines and should not be regarded as absolute rating criteria.

Dreyfus, H. L. (1989). The Dreyfus model of skill acquisition. *In* J. Burke (ed.) *Competency based education and training*. London: Falmer Press.

**This overview and scale is adapted and reproduced directly from:
COGNITIVE THERAPY SCALE – REVISED (CTS-R)
I.M. Blackburn, I.A. James, D.L. Milne & F.K. Reichelt
Collaborators:
A. Garland, C. Baker, S.H. Standart & A. Claydon
Newcastle upon Tyne, UK, 2001**

APPENDIX 2

ITEM 1 – FOCUSING ON THE PROBLEM AT HAND

Key features: This refers to the degree to which the therapist allows the client to discuss their current problem, as they see it, right now, in the session. This requires the therapist to track the current problem and its associated goals, feelings, and thoughts, and where necessary to help the client reprioritise the problem they talk about in an ongoing, sensitive manner.

These features need to be considered when scoring this item:

(i) To what degree are the problems those chosen by the client rather than the therapist
(ii) To what degree does the therapist track the problem and its features, as it is being described
(iii) To what degree does the therapist allow the client to reprioritise the choice of current problem in an ongoing manner

Mark with an 'X' on the vertical line the level to which you think the therapist has fulfilled this goal. The descriptive features on the right are designed to guide your decision.

Competence level	Examples NB: Score according to features, not examples
0	The problems are always those decided upon by the therapist rather than the client
1	The problems are only occasionally those suggested by the client
2	The problems are sometimes those suggested by the client
3	The problems are often those suggested by the client but there are examples of where the therapist makes his or her own suggestions
4	The problems are nearly always those suggested by the client but the therapist struggles to follow how they change in an ongoing manner
5	The problems are nearly always those suggested by the client and the therapist follows how they change in an ongoing manner
6	The problems are always those suggested by the client and the therapist allows the client to readjust and reprioritise their problems in an ongoing, sensitive manner

APPENDIX 2

ITEM 2 – FOCUSING ON THE CLIENT'S PRESENT PERCEPTION

Key features: This item reflects the degree to which the therapist gears the client to talk about their present experience, in the moment as it is happening. This includes current thoughts, feelings, mental imagery, memories (as they are being *recalled* right now), and current perception of the environment, including the client's own voice and the interaction as it is occurring.

These features need to be considered when scoring this item:

(i) To what degree is the session focused on present perception, through whatever modality is relevant at the time
(ii) To what degree do the therapist's questions help the client to notice the process and properties of current experience (e.g. vividness, location, timescale, pace of change)

Competence level	Examples NB: Score according to features, not examples
0	All discussion is focused on the past or future
1	Only occasionally is the content of the session focused on the present experience
2	Some of the content of the session is focused on the present experience
3	At least half of the content of the session is focused on the present experience, but many opportunities to do so are missed
4	Most of the content of the session is focused on the present experience but several good opportunities to do so are missed
5	Most of the content of the session is focused on the present experience but occasionally opportunities to do so are missed
6	The therapist takes every appropriate opportunity to focus the content of the session on the present experience

APPENDIX 2

ITEM 3 – NOTICING DISRUPTIONS AND BACKGROUND (HIGHER LEVEL) THOUGHTS

Key features: This item reflects the degree to which the therapist notices disruptions and/or facilitates the client's awareness of higher level goals, thoughts, and perceptions. Disruptions include changes in affect such as smiling or fearful expressions, changes in vocal output such as volume, pace, pausing, etc. behaviours such as gesturing, or the process of eye movement. These are detected in order to facilitate the client's awareness of them, and the goals, thoughts, and feelings related to them rather than to present the therapist's interpretations. Questioning style can also be used to facilitate awareness of background thoughts as they occur.

These features need to be considered:

(i) To what degree does the therapist notice disruptions and indicators of background thoughts
(ii) To what degree is the therapist's commenting and questioning appropriate in that it facilitates the client's awareness of disruptions and the thoughts, feelings, or goals relating to them

Competence level	Examples NB: Score according to features, not examples
0	The therapist never attempts to access disruptions or background thoughts
1	On rare occasions, the therapist asks about disruptions and background thoughts but insufficiently to allow their exploration
2	On occasions, the therapist asks about disruptions and background thoughts and sometimes this helps their exploration
3	The therapist asks about disruptions and elicits background thoughts some of the time but the way of doing so only sometimes facilitates further exploration of them
4	The therapist asks about disruptions and elicits background thoughts some of the time and on many occasions this facilitates further exploration of higher level goals and perceptions
5	The therapist asks about disruptions and elicits background thoughts regularly and on many occasions this facilitates further exploration of higher level goals and perceptions
6	The therapist regularly and sensitively asks about disruptions and elicits background thoughts wherever it seems appropriate and helpful to do so and this nearly always leads to further exploration of higher level goals and perceptions

APPENDIX 2

ITEM 4 – ASKING ABOUT PROCESS OVER CONTENT

Key features: This item reflects the extent to which the therapist's questions relate to process rather than content. The processes of particular importance involve the temporal quality of perception (e.g. when does this stop and start), the nature of changes (e.g. quick to slow), the quality of perception (e.g. vivid to faint), and whether they involve sharp or gradual differences (e.g. categorical or continuous). The process of control of perception over different timescales (e.g. sensations through plans to self-ideals and values) and to different degrees is also important (e.g. feeling little control to feeling in complete control).

This feature needs to be considered:

(i) To what degree do the therapist's questions guide the client to notice the process of their thinking, feeling, and perception in contrast to the content of thought, feelings, and perception

Competence level	Examples NB: Score according to features, not examples
0	The therapist focuses entirely on content and never asks about the processes of thinking, feeling, and perceiving
1	The therapist typically asks about content but occasionally asks about the process of thinking, feeling, and perceiving
2	The therapist typically asks about content but sometimes asks about the process of thinking, feeling, and perceiving
3	The session is about equal in terms of process versus content
4	The therapist often asks about the process of thinking, feeling, and perceiving but sometimes focuses on the content
5	The therapist nearly always asks about the process of thinking, feeling and perceiving but occasionally focuses on the content
6	The therapist takes every appropriate opportunity to ask about the process of thinking, feeling and perceiving

APPENDIX 2

ITEM 5 – MAINTAINING CURIOSITY

Key features: This item reflects the general stance of the therapist as 'curious' in a way that facilitates the client's own exploration of their perceptions and goals.

These features need to be considered:

(i) The degree to which the therapist comes across as genuinely curious and open-minded about what the client reports
(ii) The degree to which the therapist is unbiased by their own assumptions and interpretations

Competence level	Examples NB: Score according to features, not examples
0	The therapist is never curious, regularly makes assumptions and appears not to question the meaning of what the client says
1	The therapist is occasionally curious, but mostly makes assumptions and rarely questions the meaning of what the client says
2	The therapist is sometimes curious, but often makes assumptions and occasionally questions the meaning of what the client says
3	The therapist makes assumptions and shows curiosity to about an equal degree
4	The therapist maintains curiosity most of the time but sometimes makes assumptions and does not question what the client is saying
5	The therapist maintains a natural curiosity nearly all of the time and only occasionally makes assumptions or misses the opportunity to further enquire about the meaning of what the client is saying
6	The therapist maintains empathic curiosity throughout and takes every appropriate opportunity to try to understand the client and help them to clarify their descriptions

ITEM 6 – TREATING THE CLIENT WITH RESPECT AS A SOPHISTICATED, PURPOSEFUL BEING WHO NEVERTHELESS EXPERIENCES PROBLEMS

Key features: This item reflects the degree to which the therapist purveys an understanding of the client as a person with their own goals, values, and beliefs, which are respected and not oversimplified or ignored. In this context, the problems the client describes are seen as a potentially understandable consequence of the kind of life the client is experiencing, and the challenges inherent in managing conflicting values, beliefs, and goals.

These features need to be considered:

(i) The degree to which the therapist seems to appreciate the purposefulness of living
(ii) The degree to which the therapist seems to understand that goals are hierarchically organised
(iii) The degree to which the therapist seems to appreciate that internal conflict is a problem
(iv) The degree to which the therapist seems to appreciate at a human level how control is being compromised for the client; this appears to emerge naturally rather than being assumed or suggested

Competence level	Examples NB: Score according to features, not examples
0	The therapist treats the client as an object to be influenced, controlled, and manipulated
1	The therapist mostly expects the client to be compliant with demands or advice, but occasionally shows respect or consideration
2	On balance, the therapist is controlling, but shows some examples of stepping back and allowing the client to explore their own perspectives
3	The therapist is directive and makes some suggestions and interpretations, but only around half of the time
4	The therapist often respects the client's autonomy and illustrates a consideration for their predicament but some of the time makes assumptions or offers advice
5	The therapist illustrates respect for the client throughout most of the session in the way that questions are asked
6	Through their interaction, the therapist shows a respect and compassion for the client that emerges from the way the therapist regards the self-determined and purposeful nature of the client at every level

Appendix 3

APPENDIX 3

Method of Levels: common questions about the therapy

Deciding to seek help with your problem can be a big step to take. Once you have started Method of Levels (MOL), you might find that you have some questions about the therapy. Below are a few common questions that MOL clients have had, and some answers to these questions. Where relevant, we have also included anonymised quotes from people who have had MOL. If you have a question that is not covered below, please ask your therapist who will be happy to talk through any queries with you.

'What can I expect from MOL therapy?' You can expect a therapy which will allow you the time and space to talk through your difficulties. At each session you can choose whatever aspect of your difficulties you want to talk about, and your therapist will ask you questions about the thoughts and feelings you are experiencing.

'Can I bring a friend/partner/relative into the sessions with me?' MOL is all about helping people explore their own thoughts and feelings. This is most helpful for people when they can talk about their thoughts and feelings without being concerned that what they say might upset or worry somebody that they are close to. Therefore we would recommend that if you bring someone along, they stay in the waiting room while you actually have your therapy.

'How long might I need therapy for?' The amount of therapy somebody needs varies widely from person to person. For some clients, one or two sessions is enough, for other people, more sessions are required. With MOL, it is you, the client, who decides when to start and stop therapy, your therapist will not tell you how many sessions you have to attend, although different services may have certain limits on the numbers of sessions available.

'Will my therapist give me advice on how to solve my problem?' While solutions to problems are very much the focus of MOL, your therapist will not offer you advice or otherwise try to suggest what the solution might be. MOL is based on the assumption that you are the best person to bring about positive change in your own life and you are the only person who will be able to tell when the right solution to your problem is found. During the session, you will be given the opportunity to talk things through and the therapist will ask questions to help you consider your problem in a different way. Through this questioning you will be able to develop new perspectives and understandings which will contain solutions to your problems.

One client said: *'I think what I find useful is that you aren't telling me what to do, so I feel as though I'm actually making myself better. I'm changing the way I think about things but I'm able to do this myself. I'm not doing it because you've told me how to. It makes me feel stronger because I know that I'm straightening my head out myself.'*

'How might I feel at different stages of the therapy?' Some clients report having different feelings about the therapy at different stages. During the first few sessions, some people felt that they struggled with the fact that they weren't given any advice on their problem, and found it difficult to talk about upsetting things. However, as therapy continued, they came to feel as though they were making progress despite not being given advice, and began to feel more positive.

One client said: *'It took me a while to understand the MOL, after I'd had a few sessions I started to question what the therapy was all about because I felt that I wasn't getting any answers, but now I've come to understand that it's about me being able to talk in whatever way I want to, and although you don't give me any answers, you've sat there and said the right things to me and I've been able to learn the answers for myself.'*

'What kinds of questions will I be asked and why?' You will be asked questions about your thoughts and feelings as you experience them in the session. The purpose of these questions is to provide you with an opportunity to talk and think about your problem in ways that you may not have considered before.

One client said: *'The therapy has been brilliant. It's helped me a lot and it's really made me think differently about things which is something I've never done before. It's great to be able to actually think through my thoughts.'*

'I am embarrassed/ashamed/guilty/worried about telling the therapist about my problem. Do I have to tell them everything to benefit from the therapy?' You do not have to talk about anything that you don't want to. However, you may wish to talk about something without giving the therapist any details. This is absolutely fine. You don't even have to name the problem, you could give it a code name, like 'green apples' and just talk about your thoughts and feelings regarding the 'green apples'. The therapy focuses much more on the thoughts and feelings that you are currently experiencing rather than the story behind them.

'Do I have to answer the therapist's questions?' You don't have to answer the therapist's questions if you don't want to or if you feel as though you don't have an answer to give. If this is the case, the therapist might explore with you how it feels to not know the answer or to not want to answer the question, but you will never be forced to answer anything that you can't or don't want to.

'Why is the therapist asking me questions about things like my tone of voice, my facial expressions or my body language?' MOL is interested not just in what you are saying, but also in the little background thoughts that you might be having as you are talking. Sometimes these thoughts might be really important in terms of how you view your problem. Usually when we have these little background thoughts our faces or bodies give us away. We might pause, look away, smile, change our tone of voice, etc. So if your therapist asks you about any of these things they are just trying to check out if you are having any thoughts at that moment, and if so, what they might be.

One client said: *'I don't know how you pick up on it but you seem to say the right things to me and you notice my body language and any reactions or signs that I have when I'm talking. This has been important to me because it's meant that I can speak about my thoughts as they are there in my head and my mind. When you've asked me why I'm making a gesture or looking in a certain way it's made me realise what I'm doing and then as I've thought about it I've understood it.'*

'How will I feel when I leave a therapy session?' You may have a mixture of emotions following a session. Some clients report feeling good because they have been able to talk through important things, and have perhaps come to see them in a more helpful manner.

However, for other clients, talking through their difficulties can be upsetting. It is normal to feel a bit emotional after a therapy session, as dealing with your problem can be a challenging thing to do. Some clients feel a bit confused about things and some clients report being in a thoughtful, reflective frame of mind.

One client said: *'I get a lot out of the therapy; I usually leave the sessions feeling so much better than I did when I arrived. However, a few times it's had the opposite effect on me when I've left feeling worse than I did when I got here!'*

'How long will the sessions last and how often will I have to come?' Your first session will usually last about an hour although some of this time will be spent filling out questionnaires. Your subsequent sessions will last about 45 minutes, although they can be shorter than this if you wish. You can come to therapy as frequently as you want, as long as there is a free appointment slot. You can choose to come weekly, fortnightly, monthly or more than once a week – whatever suits you best.

'Why do I have to fill out questionnaires when I come for therapy?' Some of the questionnaires allow your therapist to monitor how you are feeling. For example, they might ask about your feelings of anxiety or depression over the past couple of weeks. The other questionnaires are needed as the MOL therapy is being offered as part of some research, and the questionnaires form an important part of this research.

'Why does my therapist interrupt me when I am talking?' Your therapist may interrupt you when you are talking because they are interested in something that you have just said, and want to know more about it. Your therapist might also want to know about the background thoughts that were mentioned above and, often, the best time to find out about the background thoughts is while they're actually there in your mind. If your therapist waits until you have finished what you are saying, you might not be able to remember the background thoughts that you were having a few minutes before.

As mentioned above, these are just some of the questions that previous MOL clients have asked. We hope that this information will give you an idea of what to expect from your therapy. However, if you have any further queries that are not covered here or would like any of the points explained in more detail, please mention this to your therapist who will be happy to talk things through with you.

Further resources

The following books, articles and websites provide the most relevant resources to complement this book:

Carey, T. A. (2006). *Method of Levels: How to Do Psychotherapy without Getting in the Way*. Hayward, CA: Living Control Systems Publishing. Available at http://tinyurl.com/MethodOfLevels

Carey, T. A. (2008). *Hold That Thought: Two Steps to Effective Counseling and Psychotherapy with the Method of Levels*. Chapel Hill, NC: Newview Publications.

Higginson, S., Mansell, W. and Wood, A. M. (2011). An integrative mechanistic account of psychological distress, therapeutic change and recovery: the Perceptual Control Theory Approach. *Clinical Psychology Review*, *31*, 249–259.

Special Issue of *The Cognitive Behaviour Therapist* on Control Theory. (2009). Volume 2, Issue 3.

http://www.PCTWeb.org. This website provides an introduction and links to the research and applications of Perceptual Control Theory.

http://www.youtube.com/user/InsightCBT. This YouTube channel hosts an array of videos introducing and explaining Method of Levels.

Bibliography

Aldao, A. and Nolen-Hoeksema, S. (2010). Specificity of cognitive emotion regulation strategies: A transdiagnostic examination. *Behaviour Research and Therapy*, *48*, 974–983.

Barkham, M., Rees, A., Stiles, W. B., Shapiro, D. A., Hardy, G. E. and Reynolds, S. (1996). Dose–effect relations in time-limited psychotherapy for depression. *Journal of Consulting and Clinical Psychology*, *64*, 927–935.

Barkham, M., Connell, J., Stiles, W. B., Miles, J. N. V., Margison, J., Evans, C. and Mellor-Clark, J. (2006). Dose–effect relations and responsive regulation of treatment duration: The good enough level. *Journal of Consulting and Clinical Psychology*, *74*, 160–167.

Beck, A. T. (1967). *Depression: clinical, experimental and theoretical aspects*. New York: Harper and Row.

Bennett-Levy, J., Butler, G., Fennell, M., Hackmann, A., Mueller, M. and Westbrook, D. (Eds) (2004). *Oxford guide to behavioural experiments in cognitive therapy*. Oxford: Oxford University Press.

Bird, T., Mansell, W. and Tai, S. J. (2009). Method of Levels: initial steps in assessing adherence and the development of a qualitative framework for mapping clients' control hierarchies. *The Cognitive Behaviour Therapist*, *2*, 145–166.

Bird, T., Mansell, W., Dickens, C. and Tai, S. J. (2012). Is there a core process across depression and anxiety? *Cognitive Therapy and Research*.

Bourbon, W. T. (1995). Perceptual control theory. In H. L. Roitblat and J-A. Meyer (Eds), *Comparative approaches to cognitive science* (pp. 151–172). Cambridge, MA: MIT Press.

Bourbon, W. T. and Powers, W. T. (1999). Models and their worlds. *International Journal of Human-Computer Studies*, *50*, 445–461.

Bowlby, J. (1969). *Attachment*. London: Hogarth.

Brown, T. A., Anthony, M. M. and Barlow, D. H. (1992). Psychometric properties of the Penn state worry questionnaire in a clinical anxiety disorders sample. *Behaviour Research and Therapy*, *30*, 33–37.

Carey, T. A. (2006). *Method of Levels: How to Do Psychotherapy without Getting in the Way*. Hayward, CA: Living Control Systems Publishing.

Carey, T. A. (2008). Perceptual control theory and the Method of Levels: Further contributions to a transdiagnostic perspective. *International Journal of Cognitive Therapy*, *1*, 237–255.

Carey, T. A. (2010). Will you follow while they lead? Introducing a patient-led approach to low intensity CBT interventions. In J. Bennett-Levy *et al.* (Eds), *Oxford guide to low intensity CBT interventions* (pp. 331–338). Oxford: Oxford University Press.

Carey, T. A. (2011a). As you like it: Adopting a patient-led approach to the issue of treatment length. *Journal of Public Mental Health*, *10*, 6–16.

Carey, T. A. (2011b). Exposure and reorganization: The what and how of effective psychotherapy. *Clinical Psychology Review*, *31*, 236–248.

Carey, T. A. and Carey, M. (2001). *RTP intervention processes*. Brisbane, QLD: Andrew Thomson.

Carey, T. A. and Mansell, W. (2009). Show us a behaviour without a cognition and we'll show you a rock rolling down a hill. *The Cognitive Behaviour Therapist*, *2*, 123–133.

Carey, T. A., Carey, M., Stalker, K., Mullan, R. J., Murray, L. K. and Spratt, M. B. (2007). Psychological change from the inside looking out: A qualitative investigation. *Counselling and Psychotherapy Research*, *37*, 311–324.

Carey, T. A., Kelly, R. E., Mansell, W. and Tai, S. J. (2012). What's therapeutic about the therapeutic relationship? A hypothesis for practice informed by Perceptual Control Theory. *The Cognitive Behaviour Therapist*, *5*(2–3), 47–59. doi: http://dx.doi.org/10.1017/S1754470X12000037 published online 8th May 2012.

Corcoran, R., Rowse, G., Moore, R., Blackwood, N., Kinderman, P., Howard, R., Cummins, S. and Bentall, R. P. (2008). A transdiagnostic investigation of 'theory of mind' and 'jumping to conclusions' in patients with persecutory delusions. *Psychological Medicine*, *38*, 1577–1583.

Ehring, T. and Watkins, E. R. (2008). Repetitive negative thinking as a transdiagnostic process. *International Journal of Cognitive Therapy*, *1*, 192–205.

Field, A. P. and Cartwright-Hatton, S. (2008). Shared and unique cognitive factors in social anxiety. *International Journal of Cognitive Therapy*, *1*, 206–222.

Freud, S. (1930). *Civilisation and its discontents* (J. Riviere, Trans.). London: Hogarth.

Gianakis, M. and Carey, T. A. (2011). An interview study investigating experiences of psychological change without psychotherapy. *Psychology and Psychotherapy: Theory, Research and Practice*, *84*, 442–457.

Harvey, A., Watkins, E. R., Mansell, W. and Shafran, R. (2004). *Cognitive Behavioural Processes Across Psychological Disorders: A Transdiagnostic Approach to Research and Treatment.* Oxford: Oxford University Press.

Hayes, A. M., Laurenceau, J-P., Feldman, G., Strauss, J. L. and Cardaciotto, L. (2007). Change is not always linear: The study of nonlinear and discontinuous patterns of change in psychotherapy. *Clinical Psychology Review*, *27*, 715–723.

Hayes, S. C., Wilson, K. G., Strosahl, K., Gifford, E. V. and Follette, V. M. (1996). Experiential avoidance and behavioral disorders: A functional dimensional approach to diagnosis and treatment. *Journal of Consulting and Clinical Psychology*, *64*, 1152–1168.

Higginson, S. and Mansell, W. (2008). What is the mechanism of psychological change? A qualitative analysis of six individuals who experienced personal change and recovery. *Psychology and Psychotherapy: Theory, Research & Practice*, *81*, 309–328.

Higginson, S., Mansell, W. and Wood, A. M. (2011). An integrative mechanistic account of psychological distress, therapeutic change and recovery: the Perceptual Control Theory Approach. *Clinical Psychology Review*, *31*, 249–259.

Howard, K. I., Kopta, S. M., Krause, M. S. and Orlinsky, D. E. (1986). The dose-effect relationship in psychotherapy. *American Psychologist*, *41*, 159–164.

James, W. (1890). *The Principles of Psychology.* New York: Dover.

Kelly, G. A. (1955). *The Psychology of Personal Constructs.* New York: Norton.

Kelly, R. E., Lansbergen, M. L., Wade, M., Mansell, W., Carey, T. and Tai, S. J. (2012). *Client readiness as a predictor of session by session therapeutic change: Is it important and how do we enhance it?* (Paper submitted for publication).

McClelland, K. (2004). The collective control of perceptions: constructing order from conflict. *International Journal of Human-Computer Studies*, *60*, 65–99.

McLeod, B. D., Wood, J. J. and Weisz, J. R. (2007). Examining the association between parenting and childhood anxiety: A meta-analysis. *Clinical Psychology Review*, *27*, 155–172.

McManus, F., Shafran, R., and Cooper, Z. (2010). What does a 'transdiagnostic' approach have to offer the treatment of anxiety disorders? *British Journal of Clinical Psychology*, *49*, 491–505.

Mansell, W. (2005). Control theory and psychopathology: An integrative approach. *Psychology and Psychotherapy: Theory, Research and Practice*, *78*, 141–178.

Mansell, W. (2008). The Seven Cs of CBT: A consideration of the future challenges for cognitive behavioural therapy. *Behavioural and Cognitive Psychotherapy*, *36*, 641–649.

Mansell, W. (2009). Perceptual Control Theory as an integrative framework and Method of Levels as a cognitive therapy: What are the pros and cons? *The Cognitive Behaviour Therapist*, *2*, 178–196.

Mansell, W. (2011). Editorial: Core processes of psychopathology and recovery: "Does the Dodo Bird Effect have wings?" *Clinical Psychology Review*, *31*, 189–192.

Mansell, W. (2012). The transdiagnostic approach. In W. Dryden (Ed.), *CBT Approaches to Counselling and Psychotherapy*. London: Sage.

Mansell, W. and Carey, T. A. (2009). A century of psychology and psychotherapy: Is an understanding of 'control' the missing link between theory, research, and practice? *Psychology and Psychotherapy: Theory, Research and Practice*, *82*, 337–353.

Mansell, W., Harvey, A., Watkins, E. R. and Shafran, R. (2009). Conceptual foundations of the transdiagnostic approach. *Journal of Cognitive Psychotherapy*, *23*, 6–19.

Marken, R. S. (1980). The cause of control movements in a tracking task. *Perceptual and Motor Skills*, *51*, 755–758.

Marken, R. S. (2009). You say you had a revolution: Methodological foundations of closed-loop psychology. *Review of General Psychology*, *13*, 137–145.

Miller, S. D., Hubble, M. and Duncan, B. (2008). Supershrinks: What is the secret of their success? *Psychotherapy in Australia*, *14(4)*, 14–22.

Moore, R. (2007). PRESENCE: A Human-Inspired Architecture for Speech-Based Human Machine Interaction. *IEEE Transactions on Computers*, *56*, 1176–1187.

Nilsson, R. (2001). *Safety Margins in the Driver*. Acta Univ. Ups., Comprehensive Summaries of Uppsala Dissertations from the Faculty of Social Sciences 106. Uppsala.

Patel, T. (2010). *The Development of a Scale to Measure Cognitive Behavioural Processes Across a Range of Psychological Disorders*. University of East London: Unpublished Doctoral Thesis.

Pellis, S. and Bell, H. (2011). Closing the circle between perceptions and behavior: A cybernetic view of behavior and its consequences for studying motivation and development. *Developmental Cognitive Neuroscience*, *1*, 404–413.

Plooij, F. X. and van de Rijt-Plooij, H. H. C. (1990). Developmental transitions as successive reorganizations of a control hierarchy. *American Behavioral Scientist*, *34*, 67–80.

Powers, W. T. (1973; 2005). *Behavior: The control of perception*. New Canaan, CT: Benchmark Publications.

Powers, W. T. (1998). *Making Sense of Behaviour: The Meaning of Control*. Montclair, NJ: Benchmark Publications.

Powers, W. T. (2008). *Living Control Systems III: The Fact of Control*. New Canaan, CT: Benchmark Publications.

Powers, W. T., Clark, R. K. and McFarland, R. L. (1960a). A general feedback theory of human behaviour. Part I. *Perceptual and Motor Skills*, *11*, 71–88.

Powers, W. T., Clark, R. K. and McFarland, R. L. (1960b). A general feedback theory of human behaviour. Part II. *Perceptual and Motor Skills*, *11*, 309–323.

Rollnick, S. and Miller, W. R. (1995). What is motivational interviewing? *Behavioural and Cognitive Psychotherapy*, *23*, 325–334.

Schauman, O. and Mansell, W. (in press). Processes underlying ambivalence in help-seeking: The Loss of Valued Control Model. *Clinical Psychology: Science and Practice*.

Schwannauer, M. (2007). *Cognitive, interpersonal and psychological factors influencing vulnerability, treatment outcome and relapse in bipolar affective disorders*. Edinburgh: University of Edinburgh.

Stiles, W. B., Barkham, M. B., Connell, J. and Mellor-Clark, J. (2008). Responsive regulation of treatment duration in routine practice in United Kingdom primary care settings: replication in a larger sample. *Journal of Consulting and Clinical Psychology*, *76*, 298–305.

Stott, R., Mansell, W., Salkovskis, P. M., Lavender, A. and Cartwright-Hatton, S. (2010). *The Oxford Guide to Metaphors in CBT: Building Cognitive Bridges*. Oxford: Oxford University Press.

Vancouver, J. B. (2000). Self-regulation in Industrial/Organizational Psychology: A tale of two paradigms. In M. Boekaerts, P. R. Pintrich and M. Zeidner (Eds), *Handbook of Self-Regulation* (pp. 303–341). San Diego, CA: Academic Press.

Wells, A. (2000). *Emotional Disorders and Metacognition: Innovative Cognitive Therapy*. Chichester: Wiley.
Wiener, N. (1948). *Cybernetics: Control and communication in the animal and the machine*. Cambridge, MA: MIT Press.

Index

Page references in *italic* indicate Figures and Tables.

Acceptance and Commitment Therapy (ACT) 36
acceptance therapies 54
ACT (Acceptance and Commitment Therapy) 36
action: and control 17, 18, 19–20, 25–6, 29–30, 59; and the negative feedback loop 25–6
activity scheduling 130, *131*
addiction 40
agenda setting 121–2, 127–8
alcohol 12, 40
ambivalence 36, 66, 121, 122, 123
anxiety 37, 50, 69, 74–5, 103–4, 129, 130 *see also* fear; worry; generalised anxiety disorder 9
arbitrary/inflexible control 49–52, 55–6, 69, 70, 83; and goal conflict 49, 50–1, *52*, 55–6, 69, 70, 84–5, *117*; and MOL group sessions 132

Assimilation Model (Stiles) 36
assumptions, vs questions 75–6, 89, 101, 123–4
astronomy 11–12
attention: and arbitrary control 51; to current perceptions 29, 53, 62; focusing the attention on the problem 73–7; manoeuvring attention to develop awareness 2, 79–82 *see also* awareness; selective 22
awareness *see also* attention: acute awareness of physical complaints 40; automaticity of 46; bringing higher-system contents into 53, 54; development/raising of 1, 2, 41, 51–2; of error 46–7; expansion of 13; gaining awareness of the problem 73–7; of goals 2; and imagination 45–7; manoeuvring attention to develop

167

awareness 2, 79–82; metacognitive 129; mindfulness 54, 86, 129; mobility of 45–6; of present moment perception 29, 53, 62, 83, 148; and problem resolution 47; and reorganisation 41–4, 47, 59, 62; self-awareness 1; shifting of 32, 33, 62, 79–82, 118; through questioning *see* questions/questioning; tools for focusing 53–4

Barkham, M. *et al.* 98
behavioural control 22; and perceptual control 21–4, 101; and stance 69–71
behavioural experiments 130–1
behavioural indicators 108–9, 141, 149
behaviours, transdiagnostic 7–9, 66; action and control 17, 18, 19–20, 25–6, 59; and the maintenance of distress 11–13
behaviour therapies 53–4 *see also* Cognitive Behaviour Therapy (CBT)
Bernard, Claude 25
blame, external attribution of 8
brainstorming 41
Burlingame, Gary 108

Cannon, Walter 25
Carey, T. A. 37, 73, 129, 130; and Carey, M. 136
causality: circular 58–9; of loss of control 29–30, 52, *52*
CBT *see* Cognitive Behaviour Therapy
change: behavioural indicators of 108–9; CBT techniques of 123; model of how therapy facilitates change *117*; non-linear process of *see* reorganisation; and priorities 71
circular causality 58–9
classification of psychiatric disorders 7–8, 23
Clinical Outcome in Routine Evaluation (CORE) 108
clinician effectiveness 107–9, 139–41, 145–52 *see also* evaluation, in MOL; Method of Levels Adherence Scale (MOLAS) and MOL Evaluation Forms (Self and Other)
closed loops 26, *27*, 29
Cognitive Behaviour Therapy (CBT): agenda setting 121–2, 127–8; collaborative relationship 55, 56, 128–30; control theory approach to 11–13, 65–7, 127–32 *see also* control; Perceptual Control Theory (PCT); mandated therapy 65–6; models 57–8; MOL form and practice *see* Method of Levels (MOL); terminology 11; transdiagnostic CBT based on PCT *see* Method of Levels (MOL); and transdiagnostic thinking styles and behaviours 7–9
cognitive dissonance 22
cognitive processes, transdiagnostic *see also* thought/thinking: and the maintenance of distress 11–13; self-critical thinking *see* self-criticism; and thinking styles *see* thinking styles, transdiagnostic
cognitive therapies 54 *see also* Cognitive Behaviour Therapy (CBT)

collaborative relationship: and control theory 55–6, 128–30; liberated exploration and the therapeutic relationship 115–19
collective control 116, 129
comparison, and control 17, 18, 20, 29, 59
'compulsive' people 51
conceptual models 21
conflict 35–40, 131; approaches recognising importance of 36–7; and arbitrary control 49–52, 55–6, 69, 70, 84–5, *117*; and control systems 39–40; control theory approach to 37–40; and goals 50, 51, *52*, 53, 55–6, 69, 84–5, *117*, 118–19, 121 see also arbitrary/inflexible control; and loss of control 30, 49, 53, 55; and MOL questions 123, 131; and parenting 37, *39*, 56; PCT model 37, *38–9*; and psychological distress 35–40, 49–52, 53, 84–5; and relapse 40; and reluctance to engage in therapy 40; resolution 37, 40; three-level model 37, *38–9*
control 3, 15–20, 50–1; and action 17, 18, 19–20, 25–6, 29–30, 59; arbitrary *see* arbitrary/inflexible control; without awareness of impact on long-term goals 50–1, 53, 69 see also arbitrary/ inflexible control; causes of loss of 29–30, 52, *52*; collaborative relationship and control theory 55–6, 128–30; collective 116, 129; and comparison 17, 18, 20, 29, 59; and conflict 30, 35–40, 49–52, 53, 55; control theory approach to CBT 11–13, 65–7, 127–32 *see also* Perceptual Control Theory (PCT); debilitating features of extreme control 40; directing awareness to regain flexible control 53–4, 83–8; hierarchies of 31–3, 46, 119; of input 22–4; interpersonal 55–6; and life 16–17, 20, 65, 69, 85–6; meaning of 16; MOL development of flexibility of 83–8; and negative feedback *see* negative feedback; of output 21–2, 24; overwhelming feelings of loss of 87; PCT *see* Perceptual Control Theory; of perception 21–4, 46, 62, 123 *see also* Perceptual Control Theory (PCT); perception as a process of 17, 18, 20, 25–6, 29, 59; of the present 83–5, 86–8; psychological distress from loss of 49, 52, *52*, 53, 59; questioning bringing awareness and 87–8 *see also* questions/questioning; relaxed 16 *see also* flexibility; reorganisation following loss of 42, 47, 62 *see also* reorganisation; seamless process of 85–6; *see also* stance; testing the controlled variable 133–6, *135*; utilising control theory in existing CBT 127–32
controlled variables 133–6, *135*
CORE (Clinical Outcome in Routine Evaluation) 108
core process 11–12
cost-benefit analysis 41
counter-transference 54

curiosity 89, 111, 115, 116, 151; curious questioning 75, 76, 79–81, 90, 141; and MOLAS 151; stance of 75, 115, 116, *117*, 151

decentring 86, 129
denial 66
Dependent Variables (DVs) 22
depression 43, 130
diagnostic categories 7–8, 23
disruptions 77, 129; becoming attuned to the client's disruptions 79–82; and MOLAS 149; MOL Evaluation Forms (Self and Other) 139–41
Dose-Response/Dose-Effect model 97–8
downward arrow questions 131

emotion-focused therapy 130
emotion suppression 49, 51
engagement 66
error, awareness of 46–7
evaluation, in MOL: behavioural indicators 108–9, 141, 149; evaluating your own practice 111–13, 139; forms for 139–41; MOLAS *see* Method of Levels Adherence Scale (MOLAS) and MOL Evaluation Forms (Self and Other); outcome monitoring 107–9; resources 108; through feedback 94, 107–8
exploring higher levels 32, 53, 54, 81, 105, 131
exposure therapies 54, 130
external attribution of blame 8
eye-blink reflex 58–9

fear 37, 124, 130, 131 *see also* anxiety; worry; exposure to feared stimuli 54, 130; expressions of 149; suppression of 51
feedback: negative *see* negative feedback; and outcome monitoring 107–8; questioning for 94
flexibility 2, 83; directing awareness 53–4, 83–8; MOL development of flexible control 83–8; relativity of 83; and relaxed control 16
functional models 21–2, 42, 57–8

gain 26
Galileo Galilei 7–8
generalised anxiety disorder 9
goals: and agenda setting 121–2, 127–8; and arbitrary control 49, 50–1, *52*, 55–6, 69, 70, 84–5, *117*; awareness of 2; balancing goals in the therapeutic relationship 116, *117*; brought into contact with present moment experiences 88; and conflict 50, 51, *52*, 53, 55–6, 69, 84–5, *117*, 118–19, 121 *see also* arbitrary/inflexible control; levels/hierarchies of 40, 53, 77, 83, 111, 127–8; MOL's first goal: to explore the client's problem 73–7; MOL's second goal: to become attuned to the client's disruptions 79–82; parenting 49; psychological distress from non-achievement of 1–2, 36, 50–2, *52*; questioning to identify and distinguish levels of 127–8; reorganisation of goal conflict

INDEX

see reorganisation; suppression of 40; of the therapist 111, *117*, 118, 119
Goldilocks 18
Good Enough Level (GEL) model 98
group sessions of MOL 131–2
guided self-exploration 89

Harvey, A. *et al.* 8, 9
Hayes, A. M. *et al.* 41
hierarchies of control 31–3, 46, 119
homeostasis 25 *see also* negative feedback
'How?' questions 32–3, 130

imagination 45–7
'impulsive' people 51
indecision 36
Independent Variables (IVs) 22
inflexible control *see* arbitrary/inflexible control
insight 66
internal motivation 22
interpersonal control 55–6
interpersonal styles 116–17, *117*
interruptions, by therapist 157
intrusive parenting 49

jumping to conclusions 8

Lambert, Michael 108
linear models 22
linear thinking 22

mandated therapy 65–6
Mansell, W. 12, 18, 49, 54, 88, 94, 128, 130–31
memories 85; suppression of 69–71
mental health problems *see also* psychological distress: CBT approaches to *see* Cognitive Behaviour Therapy (CBT); Method of Levels (MOL); control theory approaches to *see* control; Method of Levels (MOL); Perceptual Control Theory (PCT); and disruptions *see* disruptions; exploring the client's problem 73–7; levels of problem manifestation and generation 79, 82; PCT approach to *see* Perceptual Control Theory (PCT); willingness of client to talk about a problem 65–7; working through problems without disclosure 89–91, 156
mental states 19
metacognitive approaches 54
metacognitive awareness 129
Metacognitive Model (Wells) 37
Method of Levels (MOL) 2, 3, 54, 73; becoming attuned to the client's disruptions 79–82; client-led approach 98–100, clinician effectiveness 107–9; common questions about 155–57; controlling the present 83–5, 86–8; developing flexible control 83–8; distress focus, rather than symptoms focus 101–5; evaluation *see* evaluation, in MOL; exploring higher levels 81, 105, 131; exploring the client's problem 73–7, 147; feedback 94, 107–8; frequency of treatment 97–9; goals 73–7, 79–82; group sessions 131–2; guided self-exploration 89; information offered in first session 93–5; leaflets 94; living for the future 85–7; mindset of

the therapist 83–8 *see also* stance; outcome monitoring 107–9; quantity of treatment 97–9; questioning in *see* questions/questioning; supervision 107, 112, 113, 118–19; testing the controlled variable 133–6, *135*; therapeutic relationship, and liberated exploration 115–19, *117*; therapist's stance *see* stance; training 107, 111–13; use and relevance with other therapies and practices 117–18, 121–5, 127–32; using the past 85–7; working through problems without disclosure 89–91, 156

Method of Levels Adherence Scale (MOLAS) 145–52; asking about process over content 150; focusing on client's present perception 148; focusing on the problem at hand 147; Key Features 145–6; maintaining curiosity 151; noticing disruptions and background (higher level) thoughts 149; rating 145–6; treating client with respect 152

Method of Levels Evaluation Forms, Self and Other (Appendix 1) 139–41

Miller, S. D. *et al.* 107

mindfulness 54, 86, 129

minimisation 66

Mischel, Walter 11

models: Assimilation Model (Stiles) 36; CBT 57–8; of change and reorganisation 41–3; client-led model of MOL 98–100; conceptual 21; conflict 37, *38–9*; Dose-Response/Dose-Effect model 97–8; functional 21–2, 42, 57–8; Good Enough Level (GEL) model 98; how therapy facilitates change *117*; linear 22; Metacognitive Model (Wells) 37; model building and circular causality 57–9; nonfunctional 57–8; PCT 22; statistical 21

MOL *see* Method of Levels

MOLAS *see* Method of Levels Adherence Scale

MOL Evaluation Forms (Self and Other) *see* Method of Levels Evaluation Forms, Self and Other

motivation, internal 22

Motivational Interviewing 36, 131

natural recovery 54

negative feedback 17–18, 25, 31; homeostasis 25; loop 25–7, *27*

negative thoughts 12

optimism 43, 44, 66

OQ (Outcome Questionnaire) 108

ORS (Outcome Rating Scale) 108

outcome monitoring 107–9

Outcome Questionnaire (OQ) 108

Outcome Rating Scale (ORS) 108

overcontrolling parenting 49

parenting: and conflict 37, *39*, 56; goals 49; intrusive 49; overcontrolling 49; rejecting 49

PCT *see* Perceptual Control Theory

perception 61–2; awareness of present moment perception 29, 53, 62, 83, 148; control of 21–4, 46, 62, 123 *see also* Perceptual

Control Theory (PCT); imagination and unusual experiences of 46; internal experiences as created perceptions 102; levels of perceptual organisation 31–3; and the negative feedback loop 25–6; paying attention to 29, 53, 62; as a process of control 17, 18, 20, 25–6, 29, 59

Perceptual Control Theory (PCT) 1–2, 3, 17, 123; and activity scheduling 130, 131; and awareness *see* awareness; and the collaborative approach 129 *see also* collaborative relationship; and conflict *see* conflict; control as a principle *see* control; control hierarchies 31–3, 46, 119; and functional models 21–2, 42, 57–8; and goals *see* goals; and interventions without talking 133–6, *135*; and life as a seamless process of control 85–6; and negative feedback *see* negative feedback; and organisations 136; PCT models 22, 57–8 *see also* functional models; perception as a principle *see* perception; perception as a process of control 17, 18, 20, 25–6, 29, 59; perceptual vs behavioural control 21–4, 101; and the practice of CBT using MOL *see* Method of Levels (MOL); and psychological distress *see* psychological distress; setting conditions 65–7; sociological application 136; stance *see* stance; testing the controlled variable 133–6, *135*; utilising control theory in existing CBT 127–32; view of a client returning for therapy 125

perfectionism 40, 51, 75
person-centred counselling 54, 130
Powers, W. T. 1, 15–16, 17, 21–2, 26, 31, 42, 43, 58, 73
problems of mental health *see* mental health problems
problem solving 41; awareness and 47
psychoanalysis 54
psychological distress: capacity for 52; and conflict 35–40, 49–52, 53, 84–5; from core process from the overlapping of transdiagnostic processes 11–13; focus on distress rather than symptoms 101–5; and loss of control 49, 52, *52*, 53, 59; and the non-achievement of goals 1–2, 36, 50–2, *52*; relativity of 36; and reorganisation *see* reorganisation; resolutions through MOL *see* Method of Levels (MOL); stemming from childhood experiences 55–6; and symptoms of mental health disorders 35–6
psychosis 43, 124

questionnaires 35, 156–7; evaluation 108, 112–13, 139–40; of symptomatology 98
questions/questioning: and agenda ownership 122; vs assumptions 75–6, 89, 101, 123–4; and behavioural indicators 141; bringing awareness and control 87–8; and conflict 123, 131; curious questioning 75, 76,

173

79–81, 90, 141; and disruptions 79–82; downward arrow questions 131; explanations to a client concerning 156–7; to explore a problem 74–6; to focus on distress rather than symptoms 102–5; to gain feedback 94; homing in on present experiences 83, 85, 87, 124, 148; 'How?' questions 32–3, 130; to identify higher-level goals 127–8; MOL questioning within other therapeutic approaches 124; for MOL session evaluation 139–41; and open discussion 123; private questioning of therapists 119; to reveal ambivalence 123; and stance 71, 83–8; when the clinician is unaware of the problem 90; for when things seem stuck 125; 'Why?' questions 32, 130

recovery, natural 54
'rejecting' parenting 49
relapse 40
reluctance to engage in therapy 40, 66 *see also* ambivalence
reorganisation 41–4, 47, 59, 62, 115, 129; behavioural indicators of 108–9; how therapy facilitates change *117*; and therapist's own control hierarchies 119; through MOL *see* Method of Levels
resilience 22
resistance 116, 121, 122–3, 129
respect 66; and MOLAS 152
risk-seeking 49

selective attention 22
self-awareness 1

self-concept, and arbitrary control 51
self-criticism 12, 71; and arbitrary control 49, 51; and perfectionism 51
self-esteem 51
self-evaluation, MOL therapists 111–13, 139
self-exploration, guided 89
self-harm 51
self-identity 54
servomechanisms 15
Session Rating Scale (SRS) 108
setting conditions 65–7
speech disruptions *see* dåisruptions
SRS (Session Rating Scale) 108
stance 55, 62, 69–71, 116–17, *117*, 123–4; of curiosity 75, 115, 116, *117*, 151; and fostering a mindset in the client 83–8, 129
states, mental 19
statistical models 21
Stiles, W. B. 36
subjugation of needs 49
suicide 51
supervision, in MOL 107, 112, 113, 118–19
suppression: of emotion 49, 51; of goals 40; of memories 69–71; of thoughts 12, 83
symptoms of mental health disorders 35–6; clarifying the meanings attached to problems 102; focus on distress rather than symptoms 101–5; and personal meanings given to problems 35–6, 101–2

Tai, S. J. 128
Take Control Groups 131–2
talking disruptions *see* disruptions

Test for the Controlled Variable (TCV) 134–6, *135*
therapeutic relationship: balancing goals in 116, *117*; collaborative relationship and control theory 55–6, 128–30; and liberated exploration with MOL 115–19
therapist's stance *see* stance
thinking styles, transdiagnostic 7–9, 51; and control theory 12–13, 51, 62
thought/thinking: and awareness 45–6; and controlling present experiences 86; disruptions *see* disruptions; linear thinking 22; negative 12; parallel thoughts 79; 'racing thoughts' 45; self-critical *see* self-criticism; styles *see* thinking styles, transdiagnostic; suppression of 12, 83; thoughts 'popping' into our heads 45; transdiagnostic processes *see* cognitive processes, transdiagnostic
transdiagnostic cognitive therapy, using MOL *see* Method of Levels (MOL)
transdiagnostic processes: behavioural *see* behaviours, transdiagnostic; cognitive *see* cognitive processes, transdiagnostic; distress from core process from the overlapping of 11–13
transference 54
triggers 57, 58, 59
trying hard 50

Wells, A. 36–7
'Why?' questions 32, 130
worry 9, 40, 49, 124 *see also* anxiety; fear; being in two minds about 37; and Wells' Metacognitive Model 36–7